BACKROADS OF
SOUTHERN ALBERTA

BACK ROADS
of
SOUTHERN ALBERTA

by
JOAN DONALDSON-YARMEY

LONE
PINE

Dedicated to my family members who gave their total support and encouragement. I love you all for that. To Chevy, my four-legged travelling companion.

The publisher:
Lone Pine Publishing
206, 10426-81 Avenue
Edmonton, Alberta, Canada
T6E 1X5

Canadian Cataloguing in Publication Data

Donaldson-Yarmey, Joan, 1949
  Backroads of southern Alberta

  Includes bibliographical references and index.
  ISBN 1-55105-021-8

  1. Alberta — Guidebooks. 2. Rural roads — Alberta — Guidebooks. I. Title.
FC3657.D653 1992   917.123'4043   C92-091572-8
F1076.D653   1992

Front cover photo: *Daryl Benson*
Cover and layout design: *Beata Kurpinski*
Illustrations: *Doris Chaput*
Photography: *Joan Donaldson - Yarmey*
Maps: *Gary Whyte, Phillip Kennedy*
Editorial: *Tanya Stewart, Lloyd Dick, Phillip Kennedy*
Printing: *Best Gagné Book Manufacturers Inc.*

The publisher gratefully acknowledges the assistance of the Federal Department of Communications, Alberta Culture and Multiculturalism, and the Alberta Foundation for the Arts in the production of this book.

Contents

Acknowledgements

In researching and updating material for this book, I travelled over 13,000 kilometres (8,190 miles), covering all the paved and most of the gravelled roads of southern Alberta. I interviewed many people, in person and over the telephone, spent months reading newspapers, magazines, brochures, and books, and visited all the sites, both natural and man-made.

When I did my updating, I discovered that the province is in a constant state of change — new attractions had appeared, different roads had been constructed into some sites, while other sites had been upgraded, new craft shops had opened and a few had closed. I hope any changes since the publication of this book will only add to the adventure.

Many thanks go to the friendly people of Alberta who took the time to answer my questions, gave me directions or personally took me to hard-to-reach sites, and sent me information. Without you, this book wouldn't have been possible.

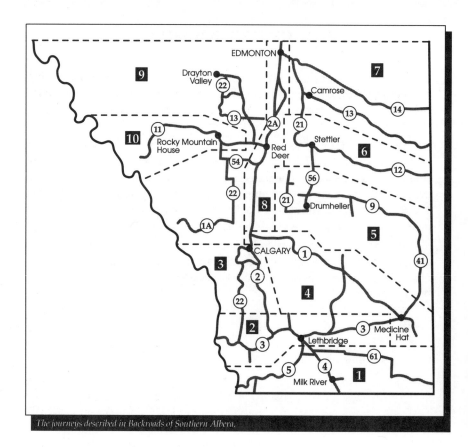

The journeys described in Backroads of Southern Albera.

Introduction

Many people, tourist and resident alike, think of Alberta in terms of mountains, Lake Louise, Banff, Jasper, the Calgary Stampede, and West Edmonton Mall. Once they have seen those sights, they head off to "more exciting" distant lands. Very few take the time to pause and see the "other" Alberta.

Alberta roads offer something for every visitor. Besides the traditional museums and historical buildings, you will find antique shops, arts and crafts shops, golf courses, ski hills, cross-country skiing trails, thousands of lakes, rivers, and streams, small and big game, waterfowl, upland birds, and the most beautiful and varied scenery for photographers and artists.

Wildlife abounds along Alberta highways. Hawks soar overhead or, on a hot day, sit on fence posts with their wings hanging down, cooling themselves. There is hardly a road that doesn't have gophers watching the traffic from the sidelines. Occasionally, deer, moose, or other large animals lope across the highway. The chatter of squirrels and the singing of birds is heard at every campsite.

With some 3,000 campgrounds and thousands of hotels and motels throughout the province, visitors should have no worries about finding accommodations for the night.

Many towns have regularly scheduled activities throughout the year including rodeos, fairs, exhibitions, and farmers' markets. Striving to keep their communities beautiful, some have painted murals on the outside walls of stores and cartoon figures or little people on their fire hydrants.

The "Princess Province" has five distinct ecological zones: grassland, aspen parkland, foothills, mountains, and boreal forest. The only landscape missing is an ocean. Not only does each zone have its own plants, insects, birds, and animals, but each also has some that are rare, unusual, and surprising.

Backroads of Southern Alberta in no way pretends to cover all that there is to see and do in this part of the province. It is designed to give you an awareness of some of the famous and infamous citizens, the natural and man-made attractions, the stories and the humour of the hamlets, villages, towns, and cities of the rest of Alberta, and to get you started on your own explorations and discoveries. It is divided into sections covering roads that share the same history or the same scenery, are in the same ecological zone, or make a nice one-day trip.

It was impossible to include all the towns on all the backroads of southern Alberta in this book, so apologies are extended to the ones missed. But just because they are not in the book does not mean the reader should pass them by. Each has its own story, or history, or site to see.

So don't hurry through our province. Stay and enjoy. And remember — many of these sights can only be seen in Alberta.

Chapter 1
Magrath to Writing-On-Stone Provincial Park

Between Lethbridge and Waterton Lakes National Park, Highway #5 passes through grassland and aspen parkland, and reaches into the mountains. The land on either side was settled by Mormons in the 1880s, and the irrigation systems and imposing churches are testimony to their past and present influence.

Highway #4 and #61 traverse Alberta's grassland. This section of the province is sparsely populated. The terrain is mainly prairie, cut by numerous coulees and river systems. Rattlesnakes, bullsnakes, western plains and wandering garter snakes, and short-horned lizards can be seen on the slopes of the coulees. Watch where you walk and don't be hasty about putting your hands into any holes you come upon.

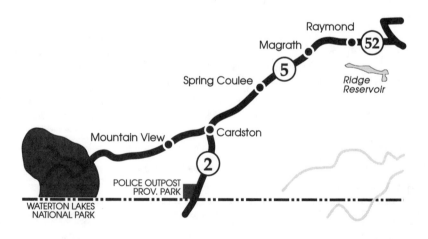

To see expansive crops of barley, canola, and oats, take the Red Coat Trail from Wrentham to Manyberries. While driving watch for yellow-bellied marmots, which are only found in the southern part of Alberta. The tall, hazy hills to the south are the Sweetgrass Hills in Montana. The wind is constant in this area.

The area around Foremost and Etzikom is excellent for viewing waterfowl. South of Foremost is the Vernon Reservoir, a Ducks Unlimited project. At the Etzikom Bird Sanctuary, you will see pelicans, ducks, geese and many other waterfowl.

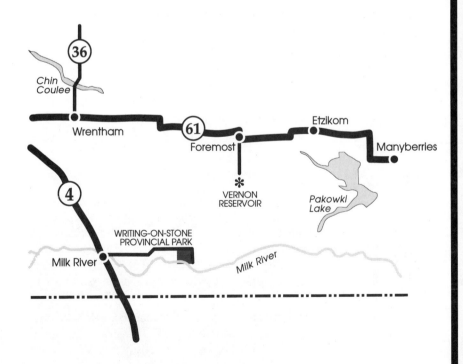

Magrath to Police Outpost Provincial Park

MAGRATH

As you near Magrath, you will see the latest concept in grain storage — the Buffalo Slope grain elevator. The green, ten storey structure, with its wide front and a sloped back, is hard to miss. Take a tour of it while you are here; it is the only one in Alberta.

Also, while in the village, stop at the monument to the Magrath Headgates. Opened in 1899, it was the first large scale irrigation system in Canada and extended for 150 kilometres (90 miles) from Kimball to beyond Lethbridge.

SPRING COULEE

Step back in time with a visit to Berry's Country Store in Spring Coulee. You will be charmed by the paraphernalia from the past arranged throughout the yard. Hitching rails, with saddles resting on the horizontal bar, line the lumber sidewalk and watering troughs lie in front. Wagon wheels lean against walls, wooden barrels are abloom with flowers, and wagons and other pieces of early farm equipment stand in the sun.

Stroll on the boardwalk and feel your steps vibrate beneath you. Inside the store you are treated to the spectacle of an antique barber chair, pot bellied stove, horse-collar mirror, wood stove, and much more. The counter top sits on old, wooden kegs and a few shelves are stocked with groceries. Be on guard for the cat. He loves to attack feet without warning.

CARDSTON

The bright white of the Alberta Temple of the Church of Jesus Christ of Latter-Day Saints in Cardston can be seen against the blue sky long before you reach the town. Overlooking its domain from a hilltop, the temple has an octagonal shape, without a definite front, and four wings that face the points of the compass. It was the first such church constructed outside the United States.

The structure is made of white granite quarried near Kootenai Lakes in British Columbia, with each 0.75 - 1 metre (2.5 to 3 feet) thick block hand-shaped before being positioned. Work was begun in 1913 and over 3,780 square metres (42,000 square feet) of granite was used before the temple was dedicated in 1923. Only those of the Mormon faith are allowed inside the building, but you can visit the interpretive centre to learn more about the temple and its history.

Mormon Temple, Cardston

The original log house of Ora Card, leader of the immigrating Mormons, is set back from the sidewalk on the west side of the town's main street. A wrought iron fence, with a gate supported by red brick pillars, extends across the front of the yard. Inside is a small museum and souvenir shop.

There are many other restored historic buildings on the streets of Cardston. For those interested in dolls, Elsie's Doll Museum is in the Carriage Lane Mall. The Cardston Museum is in the old courthouse.

Mormon Settlers and Irrigation

In 1887, 40 Mormons, under the leadership of Ora Card, fled anti-polygamy laws in the United States and established farms around present-day Cardston. The area was known for its dryness, but they were skilled irrigation farmers and soon erected a small system from the Milk River. • In 1894, the Northwest Irrigation Act was passed — those who improved a parcel of land by irrigation could claim it. The Mormons urged Sir Alexander Galt, who owned coal properties near Lethbridge, and his son Elliot to establish a method of saturating the arid land. An agreement was devised with the Mormon Church in Utah; the Galts would put up the money and the Mormons would supply the labour. The canals soon reached other communities, and in 1901, irrigation water was used on trees and gardens in Lethbridge. This was the beginning of a watering system that soon criss-crossed southern Alberta. • By 1901, 3,200 Mormons had settled in and around Cardston and Magrath.

Don Remington, owner of the Remington-Alberta Carriage Collection, once paid over $20,000 at a Texas auction for a Brewester Barouche, which he restored and added to his treasure of antique conveyances. It is now one of the over 215 carriages, worth more than $1,000,000, in his collection at 576 Main Street in Cardston. Other coaches have been donated by the Provincial Museum of Alberta, the Reynolds-Alberta Museum, and the Glenbow-Alberta Institute.

Mr. Remington began his collection in the 1950s, and at present it is one of the largest assemblages of carriages, wagons, coaches, and sleighs in North America. Other means of transportation in the collection are Phaetons, Albany sleighs, stage coaches, a Hansom Cab from 1870s England, an 1850s pumper wagon, and a 1902 school bus.

Many of the coaches have been used by visiting dignitaries, including Queen Elizabeth, Prince Phillip, Prince Charles, and the Governor General. All these lavishly restored carriages have signs, so you can read about their history as you wander around.

Cobblestone Manor, Cardston

For a treat in dining, visit the Cobblestone Manor Restaurant at 173 7th Avenue West. The building is one of Cardston's original homes and is a designated historic site. Inside, the atmosphere is serene. Heavy wooden walls are relieved by stained glass wall panels. Stained glass lamps hang over the tables, a ship's bell is at the door to ring for service, and there is a settee to relax on while you wait.

Cobblestone Manor

Cobblestone Manor was constructed by a man named Henry Hoet. Henry emigrated from Belgium in the 1910s and he had a dream. He wanted to build an elegant home for his ladylove before he sent for her to join him. Because of his job as a master carpenter at the Mormon temple, he could only work on his home in his spare time. With the help of his dog pulling a wheelbarrow, he hauled 180 metric tons (200 tons) of rock for the foundation and cobblestone walls. He used scraps of fine wood from the temple to design mosaic ceilings (one has 150 blocks, each one comprised of 61 separate pieces of wood) and he created many stained glass lights (one room has over 40 lights). • Finally, after 16 years of devoted labor, his dream was realized. Then, or so the story continues, he wrote to his bride-to-be. Instead of a joyous reply, however, his sweetheart sent Henry a "Dear John" letter. Overcome with grief, Henry spent the remainder of his days in the Ponoka Hospital and the manor was sold to pay his bills.

POLICE OUTPOST PROVINCIAL PARK

South of Cardston, on Highway #2, is the Police Outpost Provincial Park. It was named after a NWMP detachment which operated there from 1891 to 1899. Outpost Lake is stocked with rainbow trout. As you stand overlooking the lake, glance to the south and you will see the broad, flat, crown of Chief Mountain, which borders on Waterton Lakes National Park.

The park has a great number of native flowers such as prairie crocus, coltsfoot, orchids, wild chives, and lupin. Rare plants also grow here.

Prairie crocus

Mountain View

Mountain View is a tiny community consisting mainly of small businesses and souvenir shops. Caribou Clothes markets coats, slippers, mitts, hats, and other pieces of clothing made from sheep's skin. At Murray Toys and Miss Murray's Wood Shoppe, there are many different wood crafts to see.

Along the south side of the highway as you head west is a line of time-worn wagons. Though many of them are in desperate need of repair, they are still a pleasant reminder of the past.

Waterton Lakes National Park

Highway #5 ends in Waterton Lakes National Park, where the mountains rise 3,250 metres (9,750 feet) above the prairie. The lakes are a shimmering blue in the sunlight, the water in the creeks trickles over stones, and the wild animals are full of curiosity. The park has often been described as the tract "where the mountains meet the prairies," because these two topographical zones are not separated by foothills.

The Waterton valley was carved during the ice age by slow-moving glaciers. When the glaciers melted, lakes were formed, with Upper Waterton being the deepest at about 160 metres (485 feet). This body of water lies across the Canada/ United States border.

Creek in Waterton Lakes National Park

The Founding of the Park

The establishment of Waterton Lakes National Park was not easy. John George (Kootenai) Brown — a former soldier, buffalo hunter, whiskey trader, and trapper — settled at Waterton in the late 1880s. He began a campaign to have the lakes set aside as a national park, and he came close to winning his struggle in 1895 when the Kootenai Forest Reserve was developed. • In January 1901, Brown was appointed fishery officer for the reserve. But his ultimate desire was for a national park and he continued fighting for one. He was made game guardian of the reserve in 1908, and in 1910, at the age of 71, he was appointed forest ranger. He finally won his battle in 1911, when the reserve was declared a national park. However, its size was reduced to 35 square kilometres (13 square miles) and its name changed to Waterton Lakes National Park. There were 64 visitors that first year. • The park now has 525 square kilometres (203 square miles) of mountains, glaciers, lakes, and prairie, and thousands of tourists visit it each year.

As you drive into the park, watch for the sign to the grave of John George Brown, the founder of the park, along the shores of Lower Waterton Lake. A path leads down a hill and into the trees along the lake to the spot where Brown is buried between his two wives. The graves are surrounded by a white picket fence.

Mountain goats at Red Rock Canyon

While gazing at the beautiful scenery, make sure you don't miss the turn to the Red Rock Canyon. The road to the canyon is about 15 kilometres (9 miles) long and, occasionally, is very narrow. Sometimes you travel through unspoiled, open country and sometimes you hug the face of a mountain. As you wind your way up the mountainside, you will catch glimpses of Blakiston Valley. Watch for the roadside turnouts from which to see the valley and Mt. Blakiston, Waterton's highest mountain. Take a few moments and stop at some of the viewpoints — you may see a moose or deer. There are picnic areas and one camping site along the road.

At the Red Rock Canyon, a herd of mountain goats is often waiting to welcome visitors to the parking lot. As soon as you step out of your vehicle, they come over for an inspection. They do get quite close but are nervous and jump as a group when frightened. If you have a dog with you, keep it on a leash. In a head-to-head battle, the goats always win.

From the lot, you walk to a bridge and look down on the creek running over the rocks. They are red — a dull colour where they sit above the water, a bright red where the waters wash over them. You can walk down to the stream for a closer look or take a short hiking trail along the edge of the canyon. Other hiking trails, including a self-guided one to Blakiston Falls, branch out from the bridge.

Beautiful Waters

An abundance of archaeological sites show that the region was used for hundreds of years by the Blackfoot and Kootenai. It was part of a Blackfoot stronghold and the Kootenai used it for travelling through the Red Rock Canyon from British Columbia on their hunting trips in the fall. The Kootenai called the area Omok-se-kimi, meaning "beautiful waters."

As you drive towards Waterton Alpine Village, you will see the imposing Prince of Wales Hotel sitting on a bluff high above Emerald Bay on Upper Waterton Lake. The 81 room hotel was constructed by the Great Northern Railway and opened to the public in 1927. You can scan the lake and valley through the three-storey high lobby windows.

Upper Waterton Lake and Prince of Wales Hotel

Akimina Parkway, leading to Cameron Lake, is just past the turnoff to the Prince of Wales Hotel. Along the road is Discovery Well, the historic site of western Canada's first producing oil well, drilled in 1901. The parkway is 16 kilometres (10 miles) long and deer are frequently seen along it. They are surprisingly tame, so if you see one, pull over carefully, grab your camera, and climb slowly out of your vehicle so as not to frighten it. It will likely continue to graze as you snap a photo.

Park at Cameron Lake and have a picnic at one of the tables set in the trees. Or if you enjoy the water, rent a canoe, rowboat, or paddleboat. There are also fishing licenses, tackle, and bait for sale.

The water from the Cameron River cascades over some of the Rocky Mountains' oldest exposed rock at the Cameron Falls in the Waterton Alpine Village. To reach the falls, follow Evergreen Avenue to Cameron Falls Drive and turn west.

Waterton Lakes Opera House offers live theatre, cinema, and comedy. There is a swimming pool, tennis courts, a playground for the children, the Cameron Falls Interpretive Centre, and stunt-kite flying demonstrations put on by Windy Weather Kites.

Because Waterton is a peace park, the theme of the annual Beargrass Days, held in August, is international peace. There are many activities to take in, including a pancake breakfast, parade, scuba diving competition, and an open swim meet. The Peace Park Challenge is open to anyone who can form a five-member team. These teams compete in a pie-eating contest, bucket brigade, and tug-of-war.

Red Rock Canyon, Waterton Park

There are many ways to see the scenery of the park's off-road areas. Daily trail rides in July and August are offered at the Alpine Stables. For the energetic person, 190 kilometres (114 miles) of trails run throughout the park. Make sure to register with the warden at the information centre if you are going to camp overnight, and watch for bears and changes in the weather.

Hiker shuttle services to mountain trails are available at Mountain Sunset Tours. A water shuttle service to paths along Upper Waterton Lake is offered at the marina. If a water voyage is what you had in mind, register for one of the narrative cruises of Upper Waterton Lake. These tours will take you across the border into Glacier National Park in Montana.

For cross-country skiing, snowshoeing, or cold weather camping enthusiasts, Waterton Lakes National Park is open year round. There is a program of events and some services and facilities available for winter tourists.

Waterton-Glacier International Peace Park

In 1932, through the efforts of the Rotary Clubs of Alberta and Montana, Waterton Lakes National Park in Alberta and Glacier National Park in Montana were combined. President Herbert Hoover officially dedicated Waterton-Glacier International Peace Park as a symbol of the friendship between Canada and the United States. This merging also created the first universal peace park. • Although divided by an international boundary, the parks share many of nature's landscapes. The wildflowers, such as beargrass, gentian, heather, and glacier lily put on a beautiful display during the short summer. There are crowded forests of spruce, fir, larch, and lodgepole pine. Both parks abound with wildlife, including mountain goats, bighorn sheep, deer, elk, moose, black bears, and many smaller animals. Ptarmigan, osprey, Clark's nutcracker thrushes, water ouzels, and the endangered bald eagle are frequently seen here.

HIGHWAYS #4 AND #61

These two highways traverse Alberta's grasslands. This section of the southern part of the province is sparsely populated and there are few towns. The terrain is mainly prairie, cut by numerous coulees and river systems. One example of the badland formations found in this area is at the town of Foremost. Rattlesnakes, bullsnakes, western plains and wandering garter snakes, and short-horned lizards can be seen on the slopes of the coulees. Watch where you walk and don't be hasty about putting your hands into any holes you come upon.

Rattlesnake

> **Granny Cures**
>
> If you do happen to get bitten by a rattler, you want might try a "granny cure." Granny medicine has been handed down from generation to generation in prairie families. One of the remedies for a snake bite is to cut off the tail of the offending reptile and place it on the bite. After a few minutes, throw that piece away and apply another. Continue until there is nothing left of the snake. The idea of this cure is that the poison will work its way out to more familiar flesh. There is, however, no record of the success of this method. • Rattlesnakes are believed to have many healing powers. If you develop a sore throat while visiting southern Alberta, catch a rattlesnake, skin it and wrap the skin around your throat. For a headache, vibrate the rattles energetically. And to cure deafness, shake the rattles and strain to hear them.

Wrentham to Manyberries

To see expansive crops of barley, canola, and oats, take the Red Coat Trail from Wrentham to Manyberries. While driving watch for yellow-bellied marmots, which are only found in the southern part of Alberta. The tall, hazy hills to the south are the Sweetgrass Hills in Montana. The wind is constant in this area.

Wrentham and Foremost

North of Wrentham is the Chin Coulee Reservoir. The lower part of the reservoir, called Stafford Lake, has a day use area and a campsite. You can try for perch, walleye, and pike in this lake. For months in the 1920s, five well-organized gangs terrorized the banks of western Canada and northwestern United States. The groups of bandits worked out of Montana and North Dakota, with headquarters in Chicago. They pulled so many robberies that bank clerks in both countries were conducting lotteries on the probability of their banks being hit. On August 29, 1922, the Union Bank of Foremost was robbed. This robbery made front page news throughout the West.

Chin Coulee Bridge

The Alberta Provincial Police broke the case by arresting two men from the hold-up and persuading one of them to confess. With his co-operation, they recovered $860,000 which had been stolen from banks in Manitoba, Saskatchewan, and British Columbia, as well as the one in Foremost. U.S. officials eventually apprehended the remaining members of the gangs. They were convicted and sent to jail.

To this day no one knows who, if anyone, won the lottery at the Union Bank in Foremost.

Alberta Provincial Police

During the First World War, the ranks of the NWMP were depleted as men enlisted in the Canadian Expeditionary Force. By 1916, the federal government realized it did not have enough men to continue policing Alberta and Saskatchewan and it directed those provinces to form their own police forces. • On March 1, 1917, the new Alberta Provincial Police force emerged, with Major A.E.C. McDonnel as superintendent. A new uniform was designed, along the same lines as the NWMP but with a blue tunic. The force had 216 men, three cars, and a shortage of horses and uniforms. • The first year, 66 men resigned, including McDonnel, and 14 were dismissed. Under Superintendent W.C. Bryan, the APP was soon organized into an intense and strong force. Their headquarters was in Edmonton, with divisions at Red Deer, Calgary, Lethbridge, Grande Prairie, and Peace River. • Besides carrying out their police duties, the members of the APP performed many other functions: checking on homesteaders, transporting them to hospital if necessary, and looking after their affairs while they were away; distributing relief and giving out the Mother's Pension to women, with children, who were widowed or deserted by their husbands; inspecting poolrooms, theatres, cafes, cattle brands, and the cattle themselves; and collecting unpaid hospital bills, acting as game wardens, and helping the forestry department and the Indian agents. • They were diligent in their work. One annual report stated that of 2,954 arrests, there were 2,492 convictions with 19 still awaiting trial. That is a conviction rate of 89.9%. • On April 1, 1932, the Royal Canadian Mounted Police, as it was then called, assumed the role of patrolling the province once again.

The area around Foremost and Etzikom is excellent for viewing waterfowl. South of Foremost is the Vernon Reservoir, a Ducks Unlimited project. At the Etzikom Bird Sanctuary, you will see pelicans, ducks, geese and many other waterfowl. Contact the Fish and Wildlife office in Foremost for an appointment. There is a trout reservoir in the town of Foremost.

ETZIKOM

A great community effort in Etzikom has produced a windmill history exhibit on a 1.5 hectare (four acre) site at the village. Stop in and take the self-guided walk through the windmills, some of which have come from eastern Canada and the United States.

South of Etzikom is Pakowki Lake. It once drained into the Milk River but is now a dead-end system. North of the lake are sand dunes, and along the perimeter are about 150 teepee rings, reminders of a time gone by. Stone cairns, believed to be the burial ground of great chiefs, may also be found on the shore.

In this region, there is good upland bird, antelope, mule deer, and whitetail deer hunting.

As you drive towards Manyberries, watch for the Manyberries Sandhills. The village is at the end of the pavement. You can head southeast to the United States border or northeast to Cypress Hills (*Chapter 3*, Cypress Hills section). Either route will be on country roads that turn slimy when wet.

Raymond to Writing-On-Stone Provincial Park

RAYMOND

Raymond was founded by Mormon Jesse Knight and named for his son. In its founding charter, Knight decreed that if any gambling house, bar, or dwelling of ill-repute were created, the property owners would lose the title to their real estate.

Once irrigation systems were set up in this part of the province, an irrigation company sponsored Jesse Knight in his proposal to cultivate, harvest, and refine sugar beets. In 1901, 80 teams of horses plowed the fields for the next year's crop and in 1903, a sugar beet factory was opened. It operated until 1917, when it closed due to a shortage of beets.

A visit to Raymond is a must for those who enjoy historic and modern buildings. The Raymond Buddhist Temple was originally constructed as a school for Mormon children in 1902. It later became a Mormon church, then was sold to the local Japanese Society, which converted it into a Buddhist Temple.

One old Mormon church in town is made of brown brick and has two wings, each about the size of a regular church, at an angle to each other. There is a steeple in the centre and three doors: one at each end and one under the steeple. The structure sits on a large corner lot on the town's main street and is now a community centre with a performing arts theatre.

To see the house many area residents call an English castle, head west on 100th Street North. On the south side of the street is a two and one-half storey edifice with a one storey addition on the south side. Part of the house is red brick; the rest is painted white with brown trim. There are five spires or columns. It isn't really the size of a castle, but it is a very large home.

A block of Raymond's main street is so wide you can angle park on both sides or angle park down the centre. The town is the site of many provincial dirt bike competitions, which take place on a track three kilometres (1.8 miles) north of the town.

DEVIL'S COULEE

In 1987, Wendy Sloboda, a resident of Warner County, discovered some fossilized egg shells. This discovery led to a three week search by a team from the Royal Tyrrell Museum, which found a nest of dinosaur eggs at Devil's Coulee, 20 kilometres (12 miles) southeast of Raymond, on Highway #846. This notable find caused much excitement around the world. The area has been closed off, so you won't be able to drop in as you pass by. If you want to take a guided tour, contact the Royal Tyrrell Museum at Drumheller, where the eggs are now on display.

Hypacrosaurus

Along with the eight eggs found at Devil's Coulee were the bones of embryos, identifying the nest as being from a hypacrosaurus. These herbivorous dinosaurs inhabited the region about 100 million years ago and belong to the hadrosaur, or duck-billed, sub-order of ornithopods. They had small front feet and walked on their large hind ones. Although various types of dinosaur skeletons have been found in North and South America, Europe, and Asia, half of the known types of dinosaurs have been discovered in Alberta.

MILK RIVER

The town of Milk River has a centennial cairn with eight flags flying behind it. Each flag stands for a country or business that once ruled this region: Spain 1762-1800; France 1800-1803; United States 1803-1818; Hudson's Bay Company 1818-1869; Great Britain 1869-1945; the Canadian Red Ensign 1945-1965;

Milk River cairn

and the Maple Leaf from 1965. The cairn weighs 37 tons and the rocks used to build it are from across North America.

Outside the Milk River Travel Information and Interpretive Centre is a replica of a dinosaur against a backdrop of hoodoos. Inside is a small museum with a reproduction of the nest of dinosaur eggs found at Devil's Coulee.

The Milk River itself is a fascinating watercourse. Its shores are home to the western painted turtle, Alberta's only native turtle. The province's sole member of the catfish family, the stonecat, inhabits this river. This fish's pectoral fins, which have venom glands, can pierce skin and cause an unpleasant wound. The Milk River is the only major river in Alberta that flows into the Missouri drainage system, and ultimately to the Gulf of Mexico. For the canoeists, the Milk River is rated as Class 1, and it is also a popular rafting river.

WRITING-ON-STONE PROVINCIAL PARK

Writing-On-Stone Provincial Park is 31 kilometres (19 miles) east of the town of Milk River on Highway #501 and 10 kilometres (6 miles) south. It is a rugged park with hoodoos carved into sidehills, cliffs, and unusual rock formations.

The early Natives believed the area to be sacred. They recorded their existence on the walls of the cliffs and left us the largest and richest collection of Native pictographs (paintings) and

Writing-on-Stone Provincial Park

petroglyphs (carvings) in North America. Because of their fragility, the best way to see the majority of them is to book a guided tour at the tourist information booth in Milk River.

If you miss the tour, however, there is one set of carvings, protected by a large fence, that you may view on your own. When you drive into the park, watch for an "Historic Site" sign. Turn right and drive past the maintenance compound to the first parking lot. Across from the lot are three descriptive pictures on wooden pedestals and the beginning of a path down into the badlands.

The path is steep and leads to the "Battle Scene." This petroglyph portrays over 250 figures, including 115 men, 44 guns, and 11 horses, and is one of the most substantial petroglyphs in the park. Outside the protective fence is a drawing of the scene to help you pick out the characters on the rock.

To see more of the Milk River Canyon, follow Highway #501 which runs parallel to the river for many kilometres. A number of side roads will take you to the river and canyon. The gorge has some badland features, such as solitary buttes, clay flats, narrow ravines, and great vertical drops. Watch for the "dikes" — long, low, narrow walls of sandstone that have proved to be more resistant to erosion than the shales around them.

For bird watchers, over 150 species of birds inhabit the area: black-billed cuckoos, least flycatchers, mountain bluebirds, and cedar waxwings, to name just a few.

Chapter 2
Seven Persons to the Crowsnest Municipality

The highway from Seven Persons to the Crowsnest Municipality extends through one of the driest regions of Canada, but irrigation has made the growing of an assortment of crops possible. Watch for signs advertising fresh vegetables and fruit for sale. As you can guess from the strong, acrid smell that hangs over the vicinity on a hot summer day, there are many cattle feedlots in the south. Try a tour of one if you think you can handle the aroma.

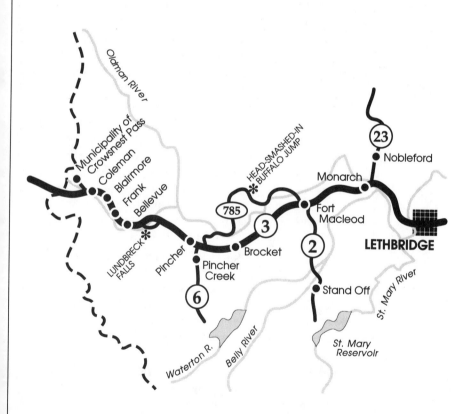

The first region in Canada to use the pivotal irrigation system was the Bow Island area. South of Bow Island on Highway #879 is the Forty Mile Coulee Reservoir. The reservoir is used to supply water to the eastern portion of the St. Mary Irrigation District. Two 28 metre (91 foot) high earth-fill dams were built 10 kilometres (six miles) apart and the reservoir between will hold up to 87 million cubic metres (936 cubic feet) of water.

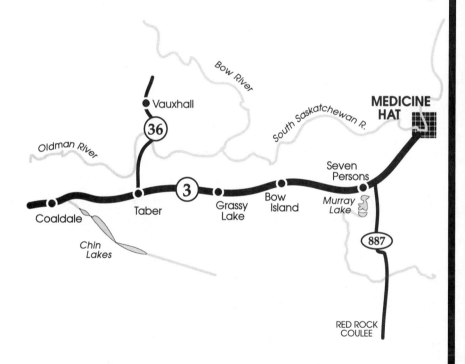

Seven Persons to Grassy Lake

SEVEN PERSONS

South of Seven Persons on Secondary Highway #887 is the Red Rock Coulee. It is one of those marvels of nature you have to see because no amount of description can do it justice.

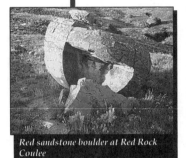

Red sandstone boulder at Red Rock Coulee

Travel 24.5 kilometres (14.5 miles) down the road until you come to an eastward curve in the highway. At the curve is a gravel road continuing south. Turn onto it and drive for about 1.6 kilometres (one mile). You will end up at the top of a hill with picnic tables and a sign explaining the area.

Before walking through the gate, stand and look down at the large masses of stone in the coulee. You will be intrigued by the huge red or reddish brown rocks that are shaped like gigantic balls with flat tops. They are scattered over a wide field and many of them have been split by the elements. While they seem to have been randomly thrown in the coulee, they are actually finely layered, red sandstone boulders emerging, through erosion, from the softer ground around them. The coulee is an ideal location for those who like to study rocks.

During the Dinosaur Age, this was a fresh water region, as indicated by ancient turtle plates, dinosaur bones, and enamelled garpike scales. The Ice Age brought reddish granite, schist, chert, and gneiss to this area.

Red Rock Coulee

Just remember as you wander through the rocks that you are in rattlesnake country.

BOW ISLAND

The first region in Canada to use the pivotal irrigation system was the Bow Island area. South of Bow Island on Highway #879 is the Forty Mile Coulee Reservoir. The reservoir is used to supply water to the eastern portion of the St. Mary Irrigation District. Two 28 metre (91 foot) high earth-fill dams were built 10 kilometres (six miles) apart and the reservoir between will hold up to 87 million cubic metres (936 million cubic feet) of water.

Below St. Mary's River Dam

When consumption is at its peak, the water is propelled by the largest pump station in Canada. Its volume of 20 cubic metres (700 cubic feet) of water per second would be enough to keep both Edmonton and Calgary supplied. Water is forced down the irrigation canals and any surplus is directed back into the reservoir for future use.

You can survey the site from a viewpoint, launch your boat, or swim in the fresh water pond near the reservoir. Pickerel, pike, whitefish, and rainbow trout are waiting for fishermen.

Irrigation

Irrigation supplies plants with water through the use of flooding, ditches, or sprinkling. Four thousand years ago, the Egyptians diverted water from the Nile River by constructing simple dams and canals. • Today, dams are still constructed on rivers to create reservoirs, and distribution canals are used to carry the water to the fields. The three main methods of irrigating land are surface, trickle, and sprinkle irrigation. • In the surface procedure, border dykes are constructed. Water is then diverted over the dykes, with small siphon tubes, from a water-filled ditch. The trickle method carries across the ground in a series of  plastic pipes with drippers, closely spaced, which trickle the water over the soil. • There are many types of sprinklers used, depending on the shape of the field. For odd-shaped fields a reel irrigator works best. A thick, polyethylene pipe, with a sprinkler at the end, is mounted on a hose reel and moved where needed. Labour is greatly reduced with the centre pivot system. The water pipe is supported above the ground and rotates on wheels around the centre water source.

Bow Island is one of Alberta's major tour centres. You can make a circuit of Alberta Sunflower Seed (9.7 kilometres (six miles) south on Highway #879), the Alfalfa Dehydrating and Cubing Plant (Highway #3, West), and the Alberta Wheatpool Bean Plant (east end of town on Highway #3). The bean plant sends 95 per cent of its bean crop to international markets such as Australia, Egypt, Sweden, England, Brazil, and the United States. This is why the town bills itself "Bean Capital of the West."

A drive down the country roads in the proximity of the town will give you an idea of the number of acres used by these industries. You can purchase packages of sunflower seeds at the Bow Island tourist information booth and you can also get recipes for tasty bean dishes.

North of Grassy Lake is the Grand Forks of the Bow and Oldman Rivers. Fisherman often cast for goldeye or sturgeon, but northern pike and pickerel can also be found in these rivers.

Taber to Monarch

TABER

Because of the extended hours of sunshine received in the district each year, Taber's motto is "Land of the Long Sun." Vauxhall, 34 kilometres (20 miles) north of Taber, once held the record in Canada for amount of sunshine in one year — 2,400 hours. The brilliance and warmth from the sun, along with the extensive irrigation systems, allow farmers to produce a number of different crops, from beans to beets and potatoes to peas.

Taber is known as "Corn Capital of Canada." Taber corn is sold throughout Alberta and parts of the United States. In the middle of August, the town holds a celebration called, not surprisingly, the Cornfest Hootenany.

Amount of Water Used

Much of the water for irrigation comes from the St. Mary's River main irrigation canal south of Taber. The Taber Irrigation District has about 383 kilometres (230 miles) of canals and about 75 kilometres (45 miles) of drains. The system uses about 100,000 acre feet of water each year. An acre foot is the amount of water needed to cover one acre (0.4 hectare) of land with one foot (30 centimetres) of water and is equal to 1,233 cubic metres (43,560 cubic feet) of water.

Willomar Arabian Stables, one of North America's top ten Arabian breeding and training stables, is 6.4 kilometres (3.8 miles) southeast of Taber. If you are a horse lover, take the time to visit the stables and see the champion, purebred Arabians. The owners of Willomar export their horses to England, West Germany, and Australia and import animals from Holland, Poland, and Russia.

If wilder animals are to your liking, drive five kilometres (three miles) east of Taber on Highway #3 to Prairie Buffalo, home to 100 head of pure-blooded bison. Besides viewing the large animals, you may also buy some buffalo meat for your supper from the owners. Buffalo meat is more nutritious than other meats, containing 25 to 30 per cent more protein and 25 per cent less cholesterol than beef.

The Taber area also offers many tours. Splash through some irrigation farms; watch your step at a buffalo farm; hold your nose at a cattle feedlot; eat your way through the Empress Foods plant; and be sweet at the Taber Sugar Factory.

Pike

If you are a person who likes to exercise and to fish, grab your rod and take the short hike to the Taber Fish and Game Trout Pond. Many lakes near Taber offer the angler a chance to pull in trout, pike, pickerel, whitefish, and ling. Goldeye and walleye can be caught in the Oldman River, but due to high levels of mercury in the water, the fish are not recommended for eating.

Mercury

Mercury is the only element that remains liquid at room temperature or below freezing. It is sometimes called quicksilver because it flows easily and rapidly. Mercury was used by the ancient Chinese, Greeks, and Romans and today is used in thermometers, barometers, and electrical switches. Mercury vapour in fluorescent lights produces light when an electrical current passes through it. One of the methods of obtaining mercury is by heating the ore cinnabar in a stream of air. Oxygen combines with the sulfur in the ore to form a gas, and leaves the mercury behind. • Mercury is poisonous and is found in our environment mainly due to pollution. Some mercury, though, comes to us from natural sources in our soils and residues. The quantity considered safe for human consumption is 0.5 parts per million, and some of Alberta's rivers and lakes have levels higher than this. Check your fishing guide for lists of unsafe fish in specific bodies of water.

LETHBRIDGE

If you are tired from travelling, stressed out from fighting holiday traffic, and hot and sticky from too much sun, a walk in

Japanese Gardens, Lethbridge

the Nikka Yuko Japanese Gardens is what you need. The gardens, on Mayor Magrath Drive and North Parkside Drive South in Lethbridge, were designed to bring peace and serenity to those who take a slow and leisurely stroll along their paths. There are no bright flowers, just green shrubs and lawn, quietly flowing waters, rock gardens, and white sand. The gardens are on 1.6 hectares (4 acres) and have five distinct

Helen Schuler Coulee Centre

sections, each offering a chance to forget the rest of the world for a while.

The gardens were designed by the City of Lethbridge and its Japanese residents as a Canadian centennial project and as a symbol of Canadian-Japanese friendship. A Friendship Bell hangs on the grounds, with an inscription indicating that if you strike the bell, good things will happen in both countries at the same time.

Indian Battle Park (Scenic Drive and Third Avenue South) marks the site of the last great intertribal fight. In 1870, a group of Cree and Assiniboines attacked a camp of Blood of the Blackfoot Confederation. A band of Peigan, also of the Confederation, came to the rescue and about 200 Cree and Assiniboine died in the clash. Except for a few minor altercations, that was the final war among the Natives. A peace treaty between the tribes was signed in 1871.

A replica of Fort Whoop-Up, the first of the "Whiskey Forts," is located in Indian Battle Park. Fort Hamilton, as it was originally called, was built by John T. Healy and Alfred B. Hamilton at the junction of the St. Mary and Oldman Rivers, the location of present-day Lethbridge. After the first fort burned in 1870, a second was constructed and became the most powerful and active in southern Alberta. The original name was forgotten and it became known as Fort Whoop-Up.

Whiskey Forts

After the Hudson's Bay Company sold Rupert's Land to the Canadian Government in 1869, fur traders from Montana journeyed into present-day southern Alberta and set up illegal trading posts called Whiskey Forts. About a dozen forts were established, one as far north as today's Calgary. Three of the more notable ones were Fort Whoop-Up, Fort Slideout, and Fort Standoff. Traders from Fort Benton drove wagonload after wagonload of whiskey and rifles up to the posts, where they traded them to the Natives for buffalo hides, wolf skins, and horses. • The structures were well fortified, with loop-holes in the walls for rifles, bars blocking the chimney tops, and doors locked against angry customers. There were small wickets in the wall through which the Native pushed his buffalo robe, wolf or fox skins, or bartered for his horses. In return, the traders presented him with a cup of "Whoop-Up bug juice," a combination of watered down whiskey and any or all of the following: tabasco, red pepper, tobacco, ginger, molasses, tea, sulphuric acid, and ink. Sometimes, a repeating rifle was given as part of the bargain to help the natives increase their hunting efficiency. • The stimulant drove the Natives wild, and they brutalized and killed their own tribesmen, other bands, and some white men. The notoriety of these forts was one of the major reasons for the formation of the North West Mounted Police.

The Helen Schuler Coulee Centre and Nature Reserve is also in the park. The reserve is situated on 78 hectares (193 acres) and has prairie, coulee, and floodplain habitat. You can take a nature walk on self-guided trails through the park, but don't expect to see trimmed green lawns or flower beds. Everything has been left in its natural state, and deer, rabbits, birds, beavers, musk-rats, and many other species continue their untamed existence in the park.

Towering over the park is the High Level Bridge, one of the

High Level Bridge, Lethbridge

largest bridges of this height in North America. It was built in 1909 and is 1.6 kilometres (1 mile) long and 92 metres (305 feet) high.

MONARCH

North of Monarch on Highway #23 is Nobleford, home of the Noble blade. During the 1930s, a drought spread over most of western Canada, and much of the top soil was blown away in the winds. Because of the extreme dryness, diverse methods of farming were put into practice and new equipment was invented.

Charles Noble, a farmer and businessman, designed the Noble blade. The cutter was used for stubble mulch tillage. It spread the stubble over the land to help prevent the soil from drifting and retain what little moisture there was in the ground.

Fort Macleod and District

FORT MACLEOD

Fort Macleod was the first post built by the North West Mounted Police in Alberta. It was constructed on an island on the Oldman River in 1874 and was named after the commanding officer. In 1875, a sawmill was put into operation, and Alberta's first drug store was opened by John D. Higenbotham in 1884.

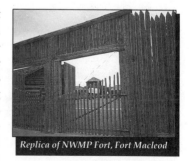

Replica of NWMP Fort, Fort Macleod

Main Street, Fort Macleod

Fort Macleod is southern Alberta's oldest settlement. The downtown district, on 24th Street between Second and Third Avenues, was declared Alberta's first provincial historical site on May 14, 1984. There are many wood frame buildings that date back to 1890s and some brick and sandstone ones from the early 1900s.

You can view the area on guided walking tours or wander around on your own. While on your stroll, watch for the plaque on the post office wall honouring Henrietta Muir Edwards. She was one of "The Group of Five" who fought for women's rights in the early 1900s.

The present-day historic buildings in Fort Macleod are reproductions, but some of the log buildings inside the Fort Museum are original and house numerous historical native and NWMP-RCMP artifacts. Don't miss the musical ride staged on the grounds every day during the summer. Young men and women dressed in NWMP uniforms present an exhibition of horsemanship and precision, similar to the world-famous RCMP Musical Ride.

Hotel Rules

Some of the men who operated the whiskey forts established legitimate businesses after the arrival of the NWMP. One of them was Harry (Kanouse) Taylor, who set up a hotel in Fort Macleod. Due to the changing times and transient population, there had to be certain rules in the hotel. They were:

1. Guests will be provided with breakfast and dinner, but must rustle their own lunch.

2. Spiked boots and spurs must be removed at night before retiring.

3. Dogs are not allowed in bunks, but may sleep underneath.

4. Towels are changed weekly; insect powder is for sale at the bar.

5. Special rates for Gospel Grinders and the gambling profession.

6. The bar will be open day and night. Every known fluid, except water, for sale. No mixed drinks will be served except in case of a death in the family. Only registered guests allowed the privileges of sleeping on the bar room floor.

7. No kicking regarding the food. Those who do not like the provender will be put out. When guests find themselves or their baggage thrown over the fence, they may consider they have received notice to leave.

8. Baths furnished free down at the river, but bathers must provide their own soap and towels.

9. Valuables will not be locked in the hotel safe, as the hotel possesses no such ornament.

10. Guests are expected to rise at 6:00 a.m., as the sheets are needed for tablecloths.

11. To attract the attention of waiters, shoot through the door panel. Two shots for ice water, three for a new deck of cards.

No Jawbone. In God We Trust; All Others Pay Cash.

On the north side of the Fort Macleod cemetery is a section for the men who died while in the force. The graves are enclosed by a white picket fence and a tall monument graces the centre of the cemetery. The oldest grave is dated October, 1874 and the youngest man buried there was 19.

Also buried in the NWMP cemetery is Jerry Potts, a guide who led troops under Col. Macleod to the original island site of Fort Macleod. He spent many years acting as a guide for the force and educating the members on survival in the West.

Golfers, here is your opportunity to play on the oldest golf course west of Winnipeg. Fort Macleod's nine hole course was opened in 1890 and has hosted many dignitaries, including the Prince of Wales in 1924. It has a club house, practice green, power carts, a ladies' par 37 and a men's 36, and measures 2,612 metres (2,856 yards). Located on the west side of town, it is just off Highway #3 along the Oldman River.

If you are looking for something different, the Great West Theatre Company presents movies or performs live productions every Friday, Saturday, and Sunday during the summer in the historic Empress Theatre. The theatre opened in 1912 and was used for vaudeville acts, minstrel shows, silent films, political rallies, and talking films. It has been renovated, but the original pressed metal ceiling, double seats in every second row, and old radiators remain.

Restored historic building, Fort Macleod

A Santa Claus parade is held in Fort Macleod at the beginning of December. It attracts more than 6,000 people from across southern Alberta, who come to take part in the festivities, which include an arts and craft show and an evening dance.

STAND OFF

South of Fort McLeod on Highway #2 is the site of the second whiskey fort to be constructed on Alberta soil. Fort Standoff was constructed in 1871. It got its name because the owners were pursued by an American marshall who did not overtake them until they were across the border. There they stopped to "stand him off."

The village of Stand Off is on the Blood Reserve and a cairn to Chief Red Crow stands as a remembrance to the mighty warrior and diplomat. Red Crow was chief from 1870 to 1900 and was one of the chiefs who signed Treaty Number 7, the last treaty in southern Alberta.

Instead of taking Highway #3 from Fort MacLeod to the towns of the Crowsnest, try the more beautiful and historic route through the Porcupine Hills. Follow #3 west of Macleod to Highway #2, turn north and drive past Alberta's largest turkey farm, where 200,000 turkeys are raised each year. The farm is famous for its smoked turkey meat. Stop and purchase some for your dinner.

Cairn to Red Crow, Stand Off

HEAD-SMASHED-IN BUFFALO JUMP

After you have travelled 4.8 kilometres (three miles) turn onto #785. As you drive down this road, you will see a wide expanse of blue-green and gold prairie with the Porcupine Hills beyond. The road is asphalt for the first 20 kilometres (12 miles) and climbs slowly into the hills. At the end of the pavement is the Head-Smashed-In Buffalo Jump Interpretive Centre.

Buffalo skulls at Head-Smashed-In Buffalo Jump Interpretive Centre

At Head-Smashed-In, you have two parking lots to choose from. The first one is at the base of the hill leading to the interpretive centre. It is paved and there is only a short climb to the building. The other lot is further out in the prairie and offers you a better opportunity to study the jump before walking to the centre. Pathways meander through the grasses to the foot of the jump where fragments of buffalo bones can be found.

Head-Smashed-In Buffalo Jump, accepted as a cultural World Heritage Site in 1981, is the oldest, largest, and most elaborate of any known buffalo jump in North America. It covers an area of 595 hectares (1,470 acres) and incorporates a variety of cultural specimens linked to communal buffalo pursuit. The remains are largely undisturbed and have provided scientists with an excellent opportunity to interpret the evolution of shared buffalo jump hunting from its beginnings 5,700 years ago to its demise in the 19th century.

Dartheads

This type of hunt was first used by Native people to kill enough buffalo for their needs. Over a number of days, a herd of buffalo was slowly lured across the prairie by drivers wrapped in buffalo hides. Others were positioned out from the cliff in a large funnel formation. As the buffalo wandered closer to the cliff, the drivers would yell to start them running. The rest waved their arms to prevent them from changing direction. As the buffalo gained momentum, the front rows could not stop at the edge of the cliff and were driven over by the rush from the ones behind.

Head-Smashed-In Buffalo Jump

Naming of the Jump

The jump received its name from a tragic incident. According to legend, one young man wanted to observe the buffalo as they plunged over the cliff. He hid himself near the base and watched as the buffalo tumbled past him. The hunt was good and as the carcasses piled up, he became trapped between them and the cliff. When his people started the butchering, they found him dead, his skull crushed. Hence the name — Head-Smashed-In.

The Head-Smashed-In Interpretive Centre is a multi-level structure built into the cliff. Each level is an artistic reproduction of a different segment of the buffalo hunt. Once you have seen the displays on each floor, ascend the final stairs for a walk along the top of the jump. The sidewalk leads to a vantage point from which you have a panoramic view of the unspoiled prairie below.

PORCUPINE HILLS

Since many animals, including elk, deer, lynx, red squirrel, and cougar, make the Porcupine Hills their home, you can expect to come upon some wildlife as you continue your journey through the hills. When you reach the Spring Point Community Hall, turn south and you will be able to see the peaks of Old Chief and the Cleveland Mountains in Montana. Continue south until you reach Highway #3 again.

From here you can turn east and drive through the Peigan Reserve, where you may buy moccasins, mitts, and other crafts at the Three Eagles Gift Shop in Brocket. Or proceed west and you will reach the Crowsnest Pass.

Pincher to Burmis

Pincher

Don't miss the Crystal Village northeast of Pincher. Over 200,000 glass telephone insulators set in cement and 900 crossarms were used to construct this miniature hamlet. The village consists of 10 buildings, including a church, school,

Crystal Village, Pincher

and coal shed. Narrow walkways connect the structures and colourful flowers and shrubs grow in the tiny yards.

Pincher Creek

South of Pincher on Highway #507 is Pincher Creek. The town received its name from a pair of pincers, a tool used for trimming horse hooves, found on the creek bank by prospectors in 1868. In 1876, the NWMP established a horse farm in the area. When it closed in 1881, many officers stayed to cultivate the land.

Many clubs and organizations have been incorporated in the town. The Oldman River Antique Equipment and Threshing Club collects and restores early farming implements in an effort to preserve the history of agriculture. In July, the club conducts exhibitions where tractors, horse powered hay baling equipment, and threshing machines are demonstrated.

Another organization is the Pincher Creek Black Powder Club. They hold annual shoots on Mother's Day weekend and Thanksgiving weekend, with the participants dressed in period clothing. The group gives black powder enthusiasts a chance to show their skills at handling muzzle-loading rifles, pistols, and shotguns.

The Willow Valley Trophy Club encourages an appreciation of wildlife, the mountains, and the river systems. It supports selective hunting of big game animals by holding a contest on the second Saturday in January. They use the Boone and Crockett scoring method for measuring the size of the horns. In addition to the awards, there are photography displays, guides and outfitters with entertaining hunting stories, and hunting gear manufacturers. Over a thousand wildlife adventurers, conservationists, and sportsmen attend every year, and many trophies have been presented for big horn rams.

The rodeo at Pincher Creek has a special section called the Cowboy Poetry Gathering. This roundup is not a competition, and it attracts poetry writing cowpunchers from Alberta, Saskatchewan, and even Montana.

Another unique aspect of the town is the Film Society's annual Indian Summer World Festival of Aboriginal Motion Pictures, which spotlights films and videos by and about aboriginal people of the world. Producers and visitors from New Zealand, Chile, Russia, Sweden, the U.S., and Canada attend the festival each year.

If you happen to be in Pincher Creek in April, May, or early June, stop in at the Hollandia Tulip Garden on Bridge Avenue. They raise over 200 varieties of tulips, hyacinths, and daffodils in all shapes and colours.

One of the historic buildings in Pincher Creek is the Lebel Mansion on Kettles Street. It was constructed in 1909 by Timothee Lebel, an early settler and founder of the largest merchandising business in southwest Alberta. The mansion is being restored and is now used as a cultural centre. You can wander through the art gallery, visit the gift shop or, if you are on an extended sojourn, attend one of the workshops on pottery, drawing, painting, quilting, weaving, or dance.

Daffodils

For the truly ardent fisherman, there are 18 high altitude lakes in the area that can only be reached on foot or horseback. Many of them, such as Grizzly and Scarpe Lakes, have been stocked with trout. But for an original experience, hike to the Southfolk Lakes (Barnaby Ridge Lakes) and fish for rare Colorado Golden Trout.

The winter sports person will appreciate Westcastle Park, Alberta's fifth largest downhill ski area. The park is 47 kilometres (29 miles) southwest of Pincher Creek. If you prefer cross country skiing, Beauvais Lake is an excellent location. Snowmobiling is very popular and many fields and trails have been set aside for the sport.

LUNDBRECK AND BURMIS

Watch for the Lundbreck Falls on the south side of the road as you travel towards Burmis. The Crowsnest River tumbles 12 metres (39 feet) to the canyon below. There is a parking lot, and a high, wire fence keeps eager sightseers away from the edge of the canyon.

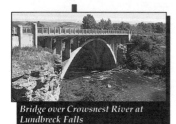

Bridge over Crowsnest River at Lundbreck Falls

If you are looking for a campsite for the night, drive across the bridge and turn east. The grounds overlook the river, and you will easily fall asleep to the soothing sound of the gurgling waters.

A short drive past the falls is the Burmis tree, a gnarled, old specimen on the north side of the highway. This is one of the few localities in Canada where this type of tree is found.

The Crowsnest Municipality

By the beginning of the century, the Crowsnest Pass was one of the largest coal producing regions in Canada. In 1898, the CPR built a line to a settlement called The Springs, later renamed Blairmore, and development began in 1901. It quickly became the centre of a coal mining area and men came from Europe and Japan to work the mines. Soon towns such as Frank, Coleman, and Hillcrest sprang up.

Crowsnest Pass

According to legend, many years ago a band of warring Crow camped close to the mountains. They concealed themselves in the rocks of the pass and waited for the Blackfoot tribe to approach. The Blackfoot warriors discovered the attackers and massacred the entire group. They then named the area "the nest of the Crows." We now call it Crowsnest.

The stone ruins on the north side of the road are the remains of the Leitch Collieries. Leitch Collieries, one of the largest coal mines in Alberta and the only one completely Canadian owned, was established in 1907. But the enterprise was short lived, and by 1915, it had ceased operations due to years of unstable coal prices. You can tour the ruins and read the displays describing the mining process.

Leitch Collieries

BELLEVUE AND HILLCREST

Approximately 356 metres (1,170 feet) of the old West Canadian Collieries' mine, also known as the Bellevue Mine, has been retimbered and stabilized and is open for public tours. Slip on one of the miners' helmets, complete with lamp, and walk the underground path the miners took to their jobs between 1903 and 1962.

South of Bellevue is the town of Hillcrest, where one of Canada's worst mining disasters occurred on June 19, 1914. At 9:30 a.m., a huge explosion rocked the mine and 189 of the 235 workers in the pit were killed.

More than 150 of the victims were buried in mass graves at a memorial cemetery in town. One grave is 61 metres (200 feet) long. The mine was soon reopened, and worked for another 25 years before closing in 1939. The Hillcrest Mine disaster occurred just 11 years after the Frank Slide.

FRANK

During the night of April 29, 1903, a wedge of limestone 640 metres (2,100 feet) high, 915 metres (3,000 feet) wide, 152 metres (500 feet) thick, and weighing 810 million tonnes (900 million tons), roared down the side of Turtle Mountain. The rock sealed the entrance to a coal mine near the bottom of the mountain, covered the valley with hundreds of feet of rock, barricaded the Crowsnest River, and crossed the valley to demolish part of the

Frank Slide

village of Frank. The slide lasted approximately 100 seconds. Of the 600 residents of Frank, the official count was 76 dead, although only 12 bodies were recovered.

To comprehend just how massive the slide was, drive up to the Frank Slide Interpretive Centre. The centre sits high above the mass of rocks and boulders and is across the valley from Turtle Mountain. See the slide presentation of coal mining life, take the self-guided tour of exhibits positioned on four levels, and stroll the boardwalk with its vista of the slide.

Turtle Mountain

The Natives had called Turtle Mountain "The Mountain That Walks" and they never camped at its base. But it was more important to the miners to extract coal from the mountain than to listen to the legend. Corridors wound deep into the mountain as the miners followed a rich seam of coal. Even when timbering crews discovered splintered props and other indications that the mountain was shifting, work continued until the side of the mountain collapsed.

The Sulphur Springs are cold springs once used by the Natives for their curative powers. They are on the south side of the highway, south of the railway tracks.

West of Blairmore is the Greenhill Mine, the best preserved mine in the area. Opened in 1913, it included a tophouse, compressor house, lamphouse, repair shop, boiler room, mine locomotives, mine shaft, timekeeper's office, hoist house, and wash house. It, too, ceased operation when the coking coal supplies in the pass were depleted. Watch for this old structure on the north side of the highway.

During prohibition, rum-running was a popular activity. One of the most famous runners was Emilio Picariello. He owned the Alberta Hotel in Blairmore and brought rum into Alberta through the Crowsnest Pass from British Columbia. He first used Model T Fords outfitted with concrete-reinforced bumpers, but later replaced them with the more powerful McLaughlin, which was nicknamed "the Whiskey Special." • Mr. Pick, as he was called, ran his business until 1922, when he and a woman friend were charged with the murder of a police officer, found guilty, and hanged. Even though he was a rum-runner, he was also a respected man in the community and there were many families who owed him for their survival during hard times.

Ninety-three million years ago, lava and ash spewed out of a vent in the Crowsnest Pass. The resulting formation is now called the Crowsnest Volcanics. It is the only volcanic rock in Alberta, and its composition indicates violent and explosive action. The rocks can be seen just past Coleman so watch for the sign on the south side of the road.

On August 2, 1920, CPR train No. 63 was robbed as it neared the Sentinel way station. Three men relieved the male passengers of money and watches and departed with about $400. One of the passengers was Mr. Pick, and he was supposedly carrying $10,000. According to the story, he slid the money under his seat and moved to another.

Five days later two of the thieves were observed in Bellevue and were involved in a shoot-out with three police officers, two from the Alberta Provincial Police and one from the RCMP. During the fight, three men were killed: one APP, one RCMP, and one train robber. The other robber fled the scene, but was apprehended on August 11. The third thief was captured four years later, when he made the mistake of pawning one of the stolen watches.

There are plenty of fishing holes in the Crowsnest Municipality. The Crowsnest River has rainbow, cutthroat and eastern brook trout, and whitefish, while Gold, Vicary, Dutch, and Racehorse creeks have rainbow and cutthroat trout. The Castle and Carbondale rivers to the south and the Livingstone and Oldman to the north all have trout.

For the hiker, there are many back country trails: one to an historic town site, another to a waterfall, a third to a cold spring, and another into the province of British Columbia. Novice and expert mountain climbers will want to tackle Crowsnest, Turtle, and Window Mountain. Photographers will use many rolls of film to capture the mountain sheep that roam along Highway #3 in the Crowsnest Pass, especially during winter and spring.

Oldman River

Chapter 3

Claresholm to Bragg Creek to Chain Lakes Provincial Park

On this route, you will make a half oval up to Okotoks in the aspen parkland zone and return through the foothills. The scenery is first-class and the attractions are numerous and unusual.

For broad vistas of magnificent scenery unequaled anywhere in Canada, turn off Highway #2 north of Cayley onto Highway #540. The Alberta foothills appear on the horizon, with the majestic Rocky Mountains towering beyond. Grass covered gullies bisect the terrain, forming miniature badlands; colourful fields of grain are interspersed with cattle grazing in pastures and the occasional farmyard. In the evening, the setting sun enhances the gold of the grasses.

In the Millarville, Turner Valley, and Longview region you can stay at one of the Equestrian Campgrounds where riding stables and camping are combined. Sheep River is great for kayaking and fishing for rainbow trout, brook trout, and Rocky Mountain white-fish. About 40 kilometres (24 miles) west of Turner Valley, on #546, are the Sheep River Falls — an excellent setting for photographers and artists.

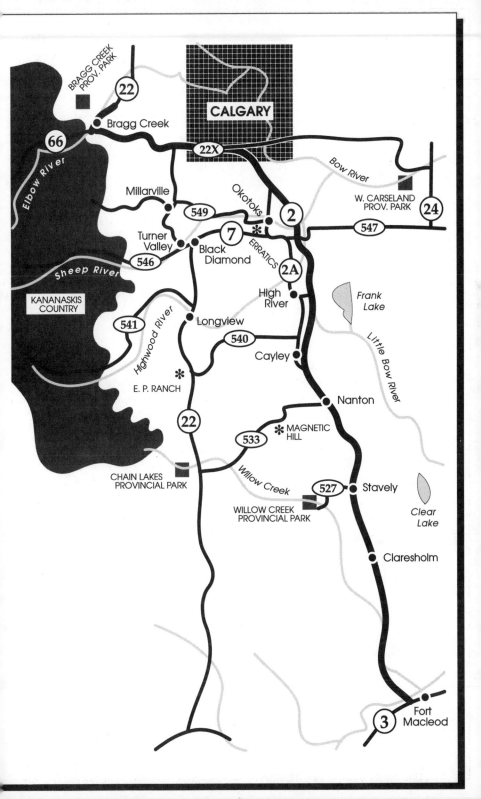

Claresholm to Cayley

CLARESHOLM

There are many large ranches around Claresholm, some of which have been in operation since the late 1800s. Besides cattle, prized Percherons and Appaloosas are also raised. Horse shows are regularly scheduled in the Claresholm Agri-plex and the town hosts the Wild West Rodeo in August.

As you drive into Claresholm from the south, you will see a statue of an Appaloosa beside the highway. One of only two museums in the world dedicated to this breed of horse is located in Claresholm. The other is in Moscow, Idaho, home of the Nez Perce Natives who bred this horse from spotted Spanish horses. The Claresholm museum, with its exhibits of books, articles, photographs, paintings, and artifacts showing the history of this "raindrop" horse, is in the James Whatt Room of the Appaloosa Horse Club of Canada.

During World War II, Claresholm was a training base for RAF pilots and, following the war, for NATO. Some of the hangars are still sound and are used by clubs in the area. The town has hosted the Canadian National Soaring Championships and national and international parachuting championships.

The Claresholm Museum is housed in an old CPR station. The sandstone station was first constructed in Calgary in 1886. By 1910, a larger terminal was needed in the city, and the obsolete depot was dismantled. Half was brought to Claresholm and assembled; the other half was taken to High River.

WILLOW CREEK PROVINCIAL PARK

Southwest of Stavely, on Highway #527, the Willow Creek Provincial Park has over 200 species of plants which are typical of a prairie valley. Some, however, such as the Douglas fir and the lodgepole pine, are not typical.

Willow Creek Provincial Park

The Douglas fir is the dominant tree in the montane (mountain) forest and is usually found on the warm, dry slopes of the foothills. Lodgepole pine thrives above the fir in the upper foothills forest. They flourish after the heat from forest fires causes their tightly closed cones to open, spreading the tree's seeds.

Other plants not commonly seen in Alberta but which are also found in this park are the sand lily, skunkbrush, poison ivy, and white evening primrose.

NANTON

The old school on Nanton's main street is actually the tourist information booth. There is a tap in the small park south of the booth. The town's water is piped from the Porcupine Hills and is so clear, cool, and clean that the town installed a drinking fountain in the park. Pause and try a sample, then fill your cooler or jug from the tap beneath the fountain.

The Lancaster Bomber in Nanton is one of the 19 remaining from the 7,374 built during the Second World War. It was restored in recognition of the men and women connected with this plane during the war and is inside the Nanton Air Museum.

To view the inside of the plane, climb a few steps, then a ladder to enter an opening under the nose of the plane. The ceiling is low, so you spend most of your time in a bent position. Signs advise you to "watch your step,

Lancaster Bomber, Nanton

watch your head" as you climb over obstructions while keeping your head down. There is much to see, including instrument panels and the gunner's seat, and two openings in the roof allow you to straighten up and stretch while you look out.

For a light lunch in a unique atmosphere drop in to the Village Smithy Tea Shoppe on 19th St. The building was constructed in the early 1900s and the blacksmith shop operated until the late 1970s. The original doors have brands burned into them from handmade branding irons. On the floor are imprints from hot horseshoes, and the forge chimney stands in one corner.

Nanton Magnetic Hill

West of Nanton on Highway #533 is the Nanton Magnetic Hill. Some visitors to the hill maintain it is an optical illusion, while others declare that nothing unusual happened to them. • If you wish to test the magnetic hill, drive until you near the 23 kilometre (14 mile) mark, the watch for the sign "Magnetic Hill 1 kilometre." At the one kilometre point, you will find yourself on a hill beside a tall, log gateway with a sign that warns "No Trespassing with Motorized Vehicles." • Stop your vehicle and study the road ahead. You will appear to be facing downhill, yet, if you shift your transmission into neutral your vehicle will back up the hill. If you don't believe it the first time, try again, then decide if it is an optical illusion.

For broad vistas of magnificent scenery unequaled anywhere in Canada, turn off Highway #2 north of Cayley onto Highway #540. The Alberta foothills appear on the horizon, with the majestic Rocky Mountains towering beyond. Grass covered gullies bisect the terrain, forming miniature badlands; colourful fields of grain are interspersed with cattle grazing in pastures and the occasional farmyard. In the evening, the setting sun enhances the gold of the grasses.

Highway #540 is paved to Highway #22. From here you can go north to Longview, south to the Chain Lakes Provincial Park, or straight west to the EP Ranch. (See the Turner Valley section in this chapter.)

High River to Bragg Creek

HIGH RIVER

High River's official insignia is the Medicine Tree. Two cottonwood trees, joined by a single branch, stood for decades near the Highwood River. According to Native legend, these trees, forming the letter H, possessed magical powers and were held in great awe. During a storm many years ago, the tree toppled but the H was left intact. To preserve the Medicine Tree, the town of High River mounted it in the George Lane Park as a display.

An excellent town for history buffs, High River has many houses, stores, and hotels that date back to the late 1800s and early 1900s. Stop in at the information booth and ask for a walking guide. Your stroll will take you past the Sam Heslip residence (built

Medicine Tree

in 1890), St. Benedict's Anglican Church (erected in 1904), and the Arnold and Arnold Law Office (situated in a building constructed in 1891).

High River's museum is in an old sandstone railway station. Just south of the station is the Highwood train project, which consists of a passenger train and a freight train. You are able to tour the various cars of each train and see the inside of a grove sleeper, a baggage car, a box car, a coach, a hopper car, a stock car, and many others. The Mail-Express car is the only restored mail car in Canada.

The dining car has been restored and now houses the Whistle Stop Cafe, a non-smoking restaurant where everything is home-made from the soups to the sandwiches. It is closed on Mondays but open for business between 11:00 a.m. and 4:00 p.m. on Sundays and 8:00 a.m. to 5:00 p.m. the rest of the week.

Because one of the major industries in the area is ranching, High River has many western shops. The antique saddles at Bradley's Western Store will give you a glimpse of the life of the early cowboy. Eamors Saddlery produces a wide variety of leather goods for sale at home and abroad. The jewellery at Olson's Silver and Leather Company is unique. Be sure to visit the Bronze Boot Art Gallery, where sculptures of western history are cast in bronze.

Lost Lemon Mine

One of the popular legends from the High River area is the "Lost Lemon Mine." The mine was discovered by Jack Lemon and his friend Blackjack in the fall of 1870. They had left Tobacco Plains in Montana in search of gold and, after weeks of prospecting, discovered a rich gold deposit near the headwaters of the Highwood and Livingston Rivers. • The men argued about whether to stay and develop their claim or stake it and return in the spring. But they fell asleep without resolving their disagreement. During the night, Lemon, still angry, stole up to Blackjack's inert form and hacked him to death with an axe. Feeling remorseful and close to losing his sanity, he returned to Tobacco Plains and confessed to a priest. Before going totally insane, he gave directions to the mine to the priest, who sent a man named John MacDougald to the scene. MacDougald buried Blackjack, marked the grave, and returned to Tobacco Plains. • Two members of a Stoney band had witnessed the murder and related the details to the remainder of the tribe. Afraid of what the gold strike might mean to their territory, they swore never to reveal the whereabouts of the mine. As soon as MacDougald left, the Natives obliterated all signs of the grave, and the claim has never been found.

The Highwood River flows just north of the town and is well known for rainbow trout, dolly varden, and Rocky Mountain whitefish. The river is also popular with canoeists and rafters.

OKOTOKS

On Highway #7 west of Okotoks is the "Big Rock," the largest glacial erratic in the world, which stands nine metres (30 feet) high, 41 metres (133 feet) long and weighs more than 16 tonnes (18 tons).

Glacial Erratic, Okotoks

The erratic is in the middle of a field on the north side of the highway and you can park in the lot provided. Grab your camera and follow the path leading to the huge rock. Children and young adults can clamber up the jagged edges while parents examine the rock and take pictures.

Erratics

During the ice age, glaciers lifted huge boulders and conveyed them along as they progressed across the land. As the glaciers receded, these huge boulders, called erratics, were left where the ice melted. Consequently, the composition of the erratics is quite different from the bedrock where they are now located. • Scientists believe the "Big Rock" was carried east by the glacial movement because its quartzite formation is identical to the composition of Mount Edith Cavell in Jasper National Park. This rock is just one of a group of erratics, known as the foothills erratics train, which stretch along the east side of the foothills.

BRAGG CREEK

Continue north of Okotoks on Highway #2 towards Calgary, then turn west on #22X to Bragg Creek. This area is renowned for its hiking and cross-country skiing, trail rides, and downhill skiing. The Bow River is a kayaker's delight.

West of Bragg Creek on Highway #66 is Camp Horizon. An outdoor camp for the physically disabled, the mentally handicapped, and the perceptually disabled, the facility offers many programs, including equal adventure, group outdoor pursuit, summer camps, winter carnivals, and workshops.

If you would like to explore the Bragg Creek Ice Caves, continue west on Highway #66 to the Canyon Creek Road, then head north for six kilometres (3.5 miles) until you come to a parking lot. Also known as the Canyon Creek Ice Caves, Moose Mountain Ice Caves, and Ing's Mine, these have "enter at your own risk" guidelines. Wear proper boots for the steep climb on the scree (loose gravel) to the entrance, and warm clothing for the cold temperature inside. Carry at least two flashlights and be cautious.

From Bragg Creek, go back on Highway #66 to #22 and turn south. For those who desire a walk through the woods, watch for signs to the Brown Lowery Natural Area, located 11 kilometres (6.8 miles) west of Plummers Road, off Highway #22. No vehicles are allowed in the sanctuary, but paths and foot bridges will conduct you through the shady forest. It is ideal for nature lovers.

Turner Valley and District

In the Millarville, Turner Valley, and Longview region you can stay at one of the Equestrian Campgrounds where riding stables and camping are combined. Sheep River is great for kayaking and fishing for rainbow trout, brook trout, and Rocky Mountain whitefish. About 40 kilometres (24 miles) west of Turner Valley, on #546, are the Sheep River Falls — an excellent setting for photographers and artists.

MILLARVILLE

Millarville was a large settlement during the oil boom and, while quite a bit smaller today, is still an active community. East of the village on Highway #549 is the Millarville Racetrack. Races were first held here in 1905, and it is the oldest racetrack in Alberta. The track is used for the races at the beginning of July, for the annual fair and for several horse shows throughout the year.

Christ Church, Millarville

Just a short distance east of the track on Highway #549 is the Christ Church, built in 1896. The distinctive feature of this church is that its log walls are in an upright arrangement instead of laying in the usual horizontal position. The church's bell is from Calgary's first Anglican Church, and the furnishings inside are a mixture of local and overseas donations.

John Ware

John Ware was one of the first black men in Alberta and a well known and respected cowboy. He was born and raised as a slave in South Carolina, and by the end of the American Civil War in 1865, he was 20, tall and strong, illiterate, and free. He travelled to Texas and worked on a ranch, where he earned a reputation as a fine horseman. In 1879, he rode on a drive herding 2,400 cattle north to Montana. After a few years of living off the land in the northern states, he joined another cattle drive into Alberta in 1882. • Ware stayed in Alberta and worked on a number of ranches before starting his own in 1891. He constructed a cabin at Sheep Creek, near Millarville. Due to his good nature and willingness to help others, John Ware was loved and welcomed by all those who knew him. • In 1902, he sold his spread and moved his wife and family to the Brooks area and a new ranch on the Red Deer River. He completed his log cabin in 1903 and, ironically, was killed in 1905 when a horse he was riding stumbled and fell on him.

West of Millarville on Highway #549 is John Ware's cairn. The cairn was erected on his original homestead at the meeting of Sheep Creek and John Ware Creek. To get to the monument,

Cairn to John Ware

follow #549 to the Bragg Creek turnoff, turn south and travel to the "T" in the road. Swing west and follow the road down a curved hill. The single-rock cairn, enclosed by a fence, is on the west side of the road.

TURNER VALLEY AND BLACK DIAMOND

In 1910, the Dingman #1 gas well was brought in at Turner Valley, signalling Alberta's first petroleum boom. Further exploration was interrupted by the First World War, and the second boom didn't occur until 1924, with the discovery of Royalite #4 near present-day Turner Valley's main street. Though gas lay underground, the topsoil in the fields was excellent for agriculture and soon cattle were grazing among the wells.

In 1899, a coal mine opened west of today's Black Diamond bridge. Coal was removed from the mine by a horse plodding around a post, which turned a drum with a cable and pail attached. Within a few years, the mine was producing 650 tons of bitumen annually. The town of Black Diamond gained its name because, at the time, the value of coal was equated with the value of the precious stone. The black diamonds weren't the only product of the mine — soot was mixed with linseed oil and used as roof paint.

Blakeman's General Store opened in an abandoned store and pool hall in 1921 and is the oldest original structure in Black Diamond. The business, still open and run by the Blakeman family, is on Highway #22, near the Black Diamond Hotel. You will enjoy a stroll through the General Store — the shelves are well-stocked and the dark, uneven hardwood floor creaks when you walk on it.

LONGVIEW

South of Turner Valley is Longview, once known as Little New York because of its rapid growth during the oil boom in the 1930s. At the village is Highway #541 into Kananaskis Country. If you follow that road for 15.4 kilometres (9.5 miles), you will reach the Sullivan grave.

Sullivan Graves

In May of 1894, three of the Sullivan family's four children, Margaret aged 6, Patrick, 2, and Peter, 14 months, surrendered to diphtheria. Their lone marker is on top of a steep knoll and their names are engraved on three of the sides.

Tearoom at the EP Ranch

Also on Highway #541 is the Tommy Bews Ranch, which attracts rodeo cowboys from around the world to its cowboy school.

Southwest of Longview is the EP Ranch, once owned by the Duke of Windsor. He bought the ranch in 1920 and maintained it for 42 years. The next owners converted his house into a tea room where guests could view trophies, ribbons, photos of prized horses, and other memorabilia in a tall display cabinet. Unfortunately, the little shop closed in 1988.

Edward definitely had a good eye for landscape. Some of the most beautiful scenery in Alberta lies just outside the ranch's door

Continue south on Highway #22 to Chain Lakes Provincial Park, where you can try your luck for some rainbow trout for supper.

Chain Lakes Provincial Park

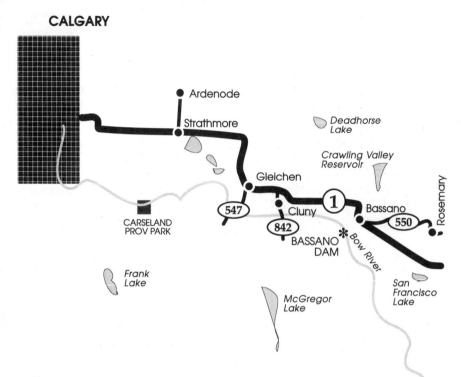

Chapter 4
Strathmore to the Cypress Hills

Highway #1, from Strathmore to Medicine Hat, begins in an aspen park area, but the scenery quickly changes to grassland. The Alberta prairie stretches for miles with little to relieve it. The golden brown of the natural grass alternates with the green of the irrigated crops.

To view dinosaur skeletons in their natural setting, head north from Patricia to Dinosaur Provincial Park. The park is situated on the Red Deer River at the southern end of the badlands.

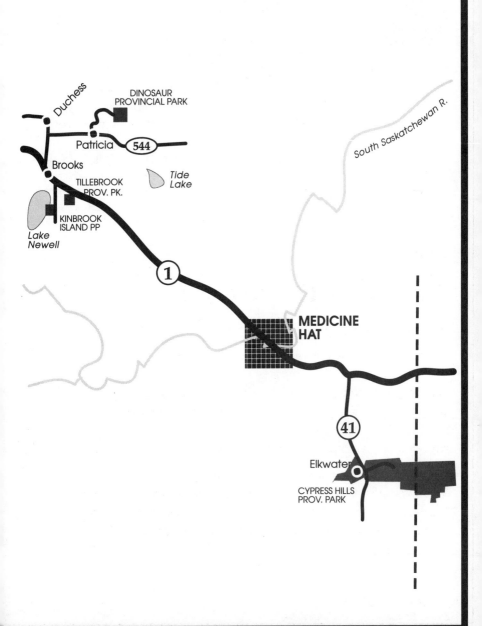

Strathmore to Bassano

Strathmore has had a long and varied history. At one time, it was the site of a CPR Demonstration Farm which supplied CPR hotels and dining cars with provisions. Between 1885 and 1904, the town was the focal point for cattle shipping from the Alberta Foothills. The Western Irrigation District began operation in the Strathmore area in 1906, and until 1910, it was the largest irrigation project of its type in the world.

The Kinsmen Lake has the lawns and trees of the Lambert and Kinsmen Parks on its shores. Seniors and children under the age of 16 can fish in the lake and walk the trails through the park.

Another establishment that has survived from the early 1900s is the Ardenode Store, constructed in 1917. To find it, go 13 kilometres (8 miles) north of Strathmore on Highway #817 to the Ardenode sign. Turn west to the Ardenode Hall, a former school in Serviceberry, then turn south and follow the road until you see the store: a small, green building, set in the trees on the west side.

Antique clocks hang on the walls, kerosene lamps sit on shelves, and an ancient weigh scale rests on the old style counter. A lovely pigeon-hole desk stands on a wooden floor covered with well-worn linoleum.

Southeast of Strathmore is Eagle Lake, named many years ago by the Blackfoot for the numerous eagles in the area. Although a forest fire in 1898 killed the resident eagles and destroyed their nesting territory, the name has remained. On the west side of the lake, Eagle Lake Nurseries has a large variety of plants suited to the Alberta climate. There is good fishing for pike and walleye in these waters.

Walleye

In the neighbourhood are Namaka and Stobart Lakes and other, smaller bodies of water.

This range is excellent for bird watching. The first record of a ruff in Alberta was made at the now-drained Weed Lake, and Alberta's first documented sighting of a black-necked stilt was west of this lake. At Namaka Lake, watch for a nesting piping plover, which has been seen in the spring.

Nearby Eagle Hill was used as a burial ground by the Cree, who laid their dead to rest in trees with the belief that it liberated their spirits.

GLEICHEN AND CLUNY

Gleichen was established in 1883 and is one of the older communities in Alberta. Watch for the many drawings on the outer walls of buildings, evidence of the Native influence in the district. The highest temperature ever recorded in Canada was at Gleichen in July of 1903, when the thermometer rose to 46° C (114° F).

If you wish to see some original Blackfoot crafts, drop into Siksika Fashions in the Siksika Commercial Complex along the highway at Gleichen. It is 100 per cent Native owned and operated and offers sweaters, jackets, sweatshirts, and other articles of clothing with Native themes.

South of Gleichen is the Old Sun Community College on the Blackfoot Reserve. The museum on the third floor traces the cultural and historical evolution of the Blackfoot tribe. The grounds of the college have been remodeled for public picnicking and pamphlets are available to help you identify herbs, bushes, and medicinal plants used by the early Natives. There are many historical sites to see while on the reserve: Chief Poundmaker's cairn, Chief Crowfoot's grave and the site of his teepee, a Whiskey Fort, and the Indian Coal Mine.

Cluny, once known for its flowing artesian wells and abundant cereal crops, was named "Grain Spout of the Bow Valley" in 1924.

For the hunters of the area, the Cluny Lions Club holds an annual Wild Game Supper in April. And for those who like to golf, drive south of Cluny on Highway #842 to the Siksika Cottage Resort on the south side of the Bow River crossing. This resort, owned and operated by the Blackfoot, has a nine hole semi-private golf course with daily rates, a clubhouse, pro shop, and snack bar.

Hong's General Store

Hong's General Store, a fixture in Cluny for many years, was used for local colour in the novel *No Fixed Address* by Canadian author Aritha Van Herk. Hong's was opened in 1916 by Louie Hong and was run by his wife and son for a few years after his death. It finally closed in 1989 and was torn down.

Bassano is famous for the Bow River dam named after. The Bassano dam, with 24 spillways, is one of the world's largest. To reach the site, follow the signs in the southeast corner of Bassano out onto a gravel road.

Bow River, down from Bassano Dam

Once you arrive at the dam, you can either cross to the other side on the single lane above the spillways or make a hairpin turn and climb a slight hill to the picnic area. While you eat your lunch at one of the tables set on the lush, green lawn, you can observe the dam, reservoir, and river. After lunch, you might want to fish or watch pelicans swimming below the dam.

For a better view, walk further up the hill to the second parking section. Large blocks of cut rock have been erected as a barrier around the outer edge. From here you can see the reservoir from another angle. In the evening, the river is illuminated by large flood lights and it is very peaceful to sit on the rocks in the dark and watch the water shimmering below.

The winds around Bassano are very strong, and the town hosts an annual windsurfing competition in the summer. Another yearly event is a pheasant hunt, which attracts hunters from western Canada and northern United States.

Bassano Dam

Brooks and Dinosaur Provincial Park

Brooks is in the centre of the Eastern Irrigation District. It is the largest irrigation district in Alberta, with 97,128 hectares (245,000 acres) of sprayed farmland and over 404,700 hectares (1 million acres) of pasture for cattle. Because of this, considerable agricultural research is conducted in the area.

The Alberta Special Crops and Horticultural Research Centre is five kilometres (three miles) southeast of Brooks on Highway #3.

The centre performs important studies on ornamental flowers, insect and weed control, plant pathology, and much more on three main farms totalling 260 hectares (650 acres). On the grounds, you can walk through many specialized areas, like the rose garden where the scent from the flowers is heavenly.

Stuffed pheasants, including a mother hen with chicks, eggs, and other displays fill the lobby of the Administration Building at the Brooks Pheasant Hatchery, a few kilometres southeast of the research centre. Informative films are shown every day for those who would like to learn more about pheasants.

Ring Neck Pheasant Hatchery

The Brooks Pheasant Hatchery is the only Alberta Government complex for raising Ring Neck Pheasants. It opened in 1945 to supplement the number of pheasants in traditional hunting areas. Each of the 6,000 hens produces an average of 40 eggs between March and June, and the facility incubates and hatches over 100,000 chicks a year. Forty thousand of these are released into the wild. • The hatchery has a raise and release program, where clubs and private landowners are given chicks to raise and turn loose on their lands. Approximately 26,000 birds each year are reared through this method.

The Brooks Museum, on Sutherland Drive, is identified by the replica of the dinosaur Corythosaurus Casuarius (alias the helmet lizard, the hooded duckbill, or the hadrosaur). The museum has many restored buildings from the early part of the century and rows of antique farm machinery.

While at Brooks, be sure to take the short drive south on 7th Street East (Highway #873) to the Brooks Aqueduct. The sight of this towering edifice sweeping into the distance on 1,000 concrete pillars will make you wonder how such an undertaking could have been achieved.

Restored building at Brooks Museum

A section of the artificial waterway over the roadway has been removed so you are able to realize the enormity of the trough and the volume of water that surged through it.

The aqueduct was erected in 1914 and at the time was the longest concrete structure in the world. Portions of it reach a height of 18.5 metres (60 feet) above the ground. It carried 18.4 cubic metres (650 cubic feet) of water per second over its 3.2 kilometre (2 mile) length and was used for 65 years before being replaced by an earth aqueduct.

Walk through the gazebos, where displays explain the use of aqueducts in Ancient Rome, the building of this chute, and the use of irrigation in Alberta. To get a better idea of the magnitude of the waterway, climb to the crest of the adjacent hill, which is actually the side of the earth aqueduct. There are more photographs outlining the construction of the modern aqueduct which replaced the cement one.

Alberta's largest man-made lake, Lake Newell, is south of the aqueduct on Highway #873. Used for water storage by the Eastern Irrigation District, it is also a favourite spot for fishing for whitefish and pike, swimming, sailing, water skiing, and wind surfing. While there, camp at Kinbrook Provincial Park, an island park with sandy beaches and shaded sites.

Brooks Aqueduct

If you enjoy watching or photographing sailboats skimming across clear blue water with their canvas unfurled, be at the boat launch on the second Wednesday of every month in the summer, when the members of the Newell Sailing Club gather for their meetings.

For the bird watcher, Lake Newell is one of the few Canadian breeding areas of the double-crested cormorant. A vast nesting population of Canada geese can also be found at the lake.

If a visit to a cattle feedlot entices you, go west of Brooks for six kilometres (3.7 miles) to Lakeside Feeders. This enterprise is one of the most extensive in Canada, with a volume of up to 25,000 head.

For those who love a good cherry turnover made with cherries and jelly, go north on #873 to Duchess then turn west and follow the road to Rosemary. The bakery and coffeeshop in the hamlet makes turnovers that actually melt in your mouth. Be sure to get there early in the morning as these delicacies disappear quickly.

Whispering Creek Petting Ranch is along Highway #554 on the way to Patricia. Drop in and let your children make friends with the exotic and farm animals, including miniature horses, llamas, pygmy goats, cattle, and peacocks. You can purchase handicrafts made by community artists or buy locally raised pets at the gift shop on the grounds.

The area around Patricia is known for its pheasant and migratory bird hunting and is earning a reputation for the bow hunting of deer.

To view dinosaur skeletons in their natural setting, head north from Patricia to Dinosaur Provincial Park. The park is situated on the Red Deer River at the southern end of the badlands.

Great Canadian Dinosaur Rush

After the discovery of dinosaur remains along the Red Deer River in 1884 by Joseph B. Tyrrell, expeditions from other countries rushed to the site and began removing skeletons, creating what became known as the Great Canadian Dinosaur Rush. • Canada's first organized entry into the badlands was in 1898 by Lawrence Lambe of the Geological Survey of Canada. He made another trip in 1901 and published a paper on the bones he found. But it was an American, Barnum Brown, who made the first effort to find and collect specimens. Over the course of five summers, he and his group found and removed 16 dinosaur skeletons, many of which were new to science. • The Canadian government did not have anyone skilled in excavating and handling the fragile remains, so they hired a professional fossil collecting family, the Sternbergs, from Kansas. They made their first visit to the area and began to collect remains for Canada in 1912.

Dinosaur Provincial Park was established in 1955, and no other region in the world has yielded as many skeletons and specimens from that era. Fossils from Alberta's badlands are housed in museums around the world, including the University of Alberta and the Provincial Museum of Alberta in Edmonton, National Museum in Ottawa, the Royal Ontario Museum in Toronto, the British Museum in London, the American Museum of Natural History in New York, the San Diego Museum in California, and the Field Museum in Chicago. In 1979, Dinosaur Provincial Park was accepted as a natural World Heritage Site.

Dinosaur Provincial Park

Stay at the park's campground and spend a few days exploring the natural preserve by guided tour, visiting the Tyrrell Field Station, hiking the trails that cross the badlands, or driving to the fossil sites.

Structures with large windows and interpretive signs have been erected near these sites to allow public viewing of staff preserving the remains.

John Ware's cabin is worth inspecting. Inside, you will find exhibits from the early 1900s: an old wood stove, a butter churn, and rustic chairs carved from logs.

John Ware's Cabin, Dinosaur Provincial Park

While Dinosaur Provincial Park is an important scientific area, it is also a home to golden eagles and prairie falcons, both endangered species.

World Heritage Sites

At the General Conference of United Nations Educational, Scientific and Cultural Organization (UNESCO) in 1972, it was decided that too much of the world's heritage was being threatened with destruction, both natural and man-made. An Intergovernmental Committee for the Protection of the Cultural and Natural Heritage of Outstanding Universal Value, called the World Heritage Committee, was formed as a division of UNESCO. Canada, the 23rd nation to adhere, joined the world heritage organization on July 26, 1976. Today there are over 100 member states and more than 300 World Heritage Sites registered with the committee. • A World Heritage Site is a location or property that is deemed to have outstanding universal cultural or natural merit. Properties which fall under the cultural site category are monuments, groups of buildings, and sites with historic, scientific, or artistic value. • Natural properties consist of physical, biological, geological, and physiographical configurations, the habitats of threatened animal and plant species, and areas of natural beauty. • Canada has had 10 heritage sites accepted since 1976. Four of them are in Alberta: Head-Smashed-In Buffalo Jump, Dinosaur Provincial Park, Wood Buffalo National Park, and the combined Banff and Jasper National Parks .

Medicine Hat and District

MEDICINE HAT

Rudyard Kipling dubbed Medicine Hat "the city with all hell for a basement" because of the gas fields discovered beneath it in 1885. By 1890, the homes, offices, schools, and churches of the town were being heated by gas.

The City of Medicine Hat offers a half-hour walking tour of its historic downtown. On the tour, you will see St. Patrick's Church, one of the finest examples of Gothic Revival architecture in North America. Construction of the church, with its 52 metre (170 feet) high Gothic towers, demanded a continuous pouring of concrete from the foundation to the crosses at the top.

The oldest brick residence still standing in Alberta is the Ewart/ Duggan Home in Medicine Hat. It was built by John Ewart in 1887 and has remained basically unchanged since then. Even the roof is still protected by the original cedar shingles.

In contrast with the distinguished older buildings of Medicine Hat is the City Hall. It is a mixture of red brick, glass, and shiny metal set high on the banks of the South Saskatchewan River.

Medalta Potteries

For many years Medicine Hat was well-known for its pottery. Medalta Potteries, established in 1912, produced a variety of earthenware — from wine jugs for the liquor control boards of the three prairie provinces to lamp bases and decorative artware. It furnished the CNR, the CPR, and many large hotels with all their dinnerware. During the Second World War, it supplied dishes for Canadian troops. • Medalta Potteries was the first Western company to ship manufactured goods to eastern Canada and the first to employ a female factory supervisor. Because of mismanagement, the business slowly declined and ceased operation in the 1950s. Today, Medalta pottery is sought after by collectors around the world.

There are many parks inside and outside the city where you can stroll, jog, or cycle in summer and cross-country ski in winter.

On the north side of the Saskatchewan River are several beautiful tree-lined streets. Heavy branches hang over these thoroughfares, leaving some of them almost completely in shade. Second and Third Streets, northwest, are two fine examples.

For the young and the young-at-heart there is the Riverside Waterslide. Western Canada's largest waterslide offers night sliding on Fridays and many events during the summer such as sack races, volleyball games, and pie-eating contests.

Fifth Avenue United Church, Medecine Hat

Medicine Hat is the home of the Toronto Blue Jays farm team, who play regularly scheduled games throughout the season. You might want to take in a game while in the city.

Fay Wray, though raised in Los Angeles, was born in Medicine Hat in 1907. She appeared in many films but is best remembered for her portrayal of the heroine and love interest in the original version of *King Kong*.

The South Saskatchewan River at Medicine Hat is good for catching sturgeon, northern pike, pickerel, and goldeye. If you fancy trout, try Echo Dale Park.

Redcliff, just northwest of Medicine Hat, is home to Redcliff Greenhouses. The operation is the largest in the prairie provinces, made up of one hectare (2.5 acres) of flowers and plants under glass. It is open all year, and tours are available.

From Medicine Hat, go east along Highway #1 to Highway #41 and turn south towards the Cypress Hills. The drive is through flat prairie relieved by a few knolls until suddenly, in the distance, the green forested Cypress Hills rise above the grassland.

Cypress Hills

The Cypress Hills are the oldest hill lands in Alberta, dating back 50 million years, and have the highest elevation in Canada between the Rocky Mountains and the east coast. They were formed by a build up of sediment from an ancient sea and from materials deposited by large rivers. Because of their composition, they resisted erosion considerably better than the remainder of the region. • When the glaciers advanced over the land thousands of years ago, they did not totally envelop the 1462 m (4810 ft) high hills. A nunatak, or area of land, was left protruding above the glacial ice. • The Blackfoot called the area "Katehuis Netumoo" which means Sweet Pine Hills. When the French fur traders arrived, they mistook the lodgepole pine in the hills for their eastern Jackpine and named them "Montagne de Cypres" meaning Jack Pine Mountains. Through the English translation, the hills became known as the Cypress Hills even though Cypress trees have never grown there. • Because of their altitude, the climate of the hills is much cooler and more humid than the surrounding prairie. There is enough rainfall in this surrounding plains or steppe section of the grasslands to prevent desert but not enough to grow trees.

Cypress Hills Provincial Park, at 200 square kilometres (124 square miles), is Alberta's second largest park. Thirteen different campgrounds, with 530 sites, range from walk-in tenting to fully serviced plots. Try one of the many hiking trails, swim in one of the lakes, or rent a bicycle in Elkwater for a tour. In winter, you are able to icefish, downhill ski, cross-country ski, and snowshoe on the 25 kilometres (15.5 miles) of trails.

Cypress Hills Provincial Park

Stop in at the visitor centre in Elkwater for a map of the park, then follow Highway #41 to the top of the hills. Various roads criss-cross the park and each one has something of interest to see. As you tour, watch for free-roaming herds of cattle and horses.

At the first crossroads, turn east and drive to the Bull Trail sign. Look behind the sign and you will see the faint indentation left by the wooden wheels of wagons travelling between Fort Benton, Montana and Fort Macleod, Alberta over a hundred years ago.

From this sign you can turn onto the Bull Trail, a narrow, winding, and sometimes steep gravel road, and drive to Spruce Coulee where only non-powered watercraft are allowed on the waters of the reservoir. Or you can continue east to the Reesor

Survival Tree, Cypress Hills

Lake Viewpoint. Cross the highway and climb the small hill for a look at the road which winds below. Follow the road to Reesor Lake itself, where you can use boats with electric motors when fishing for rainbow trout.

Further east is the Graburn cairn, dedicated to the first NWMP officer to be killed on duty. Constable Marmaduke Graburn was murdered on November 17, 1879 in the Cypress Hills, and his killers were never caught.

At the cairn turn south on Graburn Road and drive to a solitary, misshapen tree surrounded by a white, metal fence. Called the Survival Tree, it has withstood nature's and man's assault on it for over 100 years. The wind has blown it, snows have fallen on it, the sun has dried it, and cattle have abused it. In 1900, an attempt was made to chop it down, but still it endures.

West of Highway #41 on the Murray Hill Road is the Horseshoe Canyon Viewpoint, which overlooks a large slide. It was caused by water freezing in cracks in the ground, which finally weakened and slid into the valley below.

The Head of the Mountain Métis site, a buffalo hinting community from the 1870s, is located at the west end of the park.

Wildlife in the Cypress Hills

While driving through the park watch for the many varieties of flowers, different species of wildlife, and the over 200 types of birds. Sixteen species of orchids grow in the park. One type, White Adder's Mouth (*Malaxis monophylla*) has only been discovered in six locations in Alberta. Alberta's only native turtle, the western painted turtle, is found in the Cypress Hills and along the Milk River. • Elk were reintroduced in 1938 to replace the herds hunted to extinction in 1909. In the mid-1950s, moose were brought to the hills, and in 1962, wild turkeys, though not native, were established.

If you want to observe a plant and insect combination that can only be seen in a handful of places in Canada, take Highway #41 south to #502. Turn west toward Onefor and travel past the hamlet for 10 kilometres (six miles). In this area you will see soapweed, a species of yucca. Fluttering near this plant you might find a rare yucca moth.

Just a word of caution. The roads in this area are extremely hazardous when wet. The high bentonite content in the soft bedrock makes paths and lanes slimy.

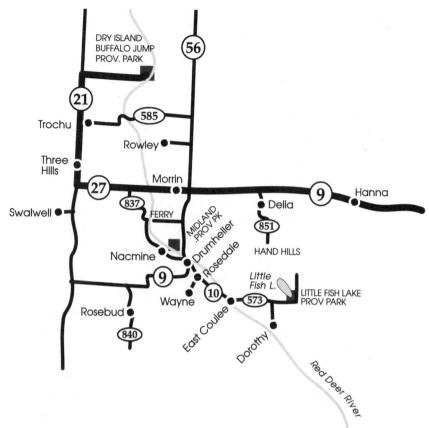

Chapter 5

Middle Sand Hills to the Dry Island Buffalo Jump Provincial Park

On this drive, you will travel through a very hot, windy, arid, but picturesque zone of Alberta. The scenery encompasses sand dunes, hills, and badlands, as well as rivers and lakes. And you never know when you might see a pronghorn or some other wild animal, so keep your camera handy.

The Middle Sand Hills between Medicine Hat and Empress are dunes that, for the most part, have been stabilized by prairie vegetation. Some shifting of the sands, however, continues north of Hilda and south of the South Saskatchewan River.

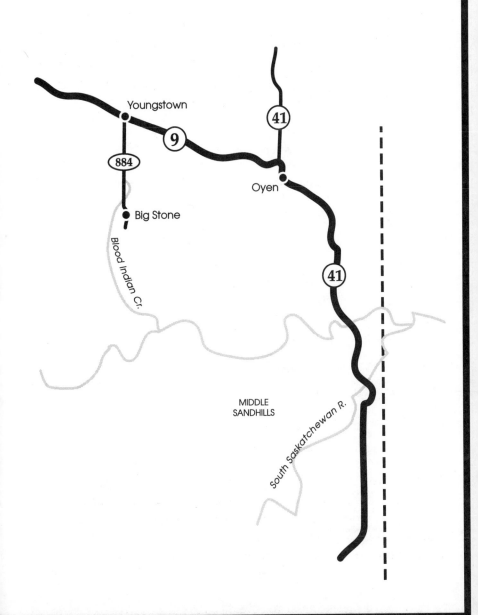

Middle Sand Hills to Hanna

MIDDLE SAND HILLS

The Middle Sand Hills between Medicine Hat and Empress are dunes that, for the most part, have been stabilized by prairie vegetation. Some shifting of the sands, however, continues north of Hilda and south of the South Saskatchewan River.

The sand hills are a popular habitat for unusual species of insects, plants, and birds. Two rare classifications of the tiger beetle, *Cicindella nevadica* and *Cicindella fulgida*, have been discovered exclusively in this part of Alberta. A desert variety of plant, the sand verbena, seldom seen this far north, has been identified in the hills. As well, a western sandpiper has been sighted.

As you drive over the two major rivers in the region, study how the rivers have eroded the surrounding terrain. The South Saskatchewan, formed by the convergence of the Bow and Oldman Rivers, has gouged a deep, narrow valley while the Red Deer, 20 kilometres (12 miles) to the north, is broad and flows virtually level with the surrounding plains.

OYEN

Because of the large number of pronghorn in the area, Oyen has adopted the animal as its emblem. A replica of a pronghorn can be found in the park by the grain elevators.

The Pronghorn

Although it has been called the American antelope, the pronghorn has no close family members. It is, however, a cud-chewing mammal similar to the antelope. This agile animal has a stocky body on slender legs, large pointed ears, and a short tail. Its horns grow to about 35 centimetres (14 inches) long and are composed of a centre bone covered by a dark, hardened layer. This outer cover is discarded every year, leaving the core intact — the pronghorn is the only animal in the world that sheds its horn protection. • The pronghorn is well suited to its grassland environment. It has telescopic eyesight and can detect movement a mile away. To dissipate the heat of the summer, it uses an open-mouth panting system, while hollow hairs keeps it warm in the winter. When startled, it can leap 4.6 metres (15 feet) in one bound and travel up to 100 kilometres per hour (60 miles per hour) in a short sprint. Pronghorns have been known to run at a rate of 64 kilometres per hour (40 miles per hour) for up to three kilometres (two miles). • At one time, the pronghorn numbered 100 million; now there are only an estimated 250,000 left.

Turn west onto Highway #9, and when you reach Youngstown take Highway #884 30 kilometres (18 miles) south to Big Stone and Blood Indian Park. By damming the Blood Indian Creek, the band has created a large lake and transformed the prairie into a lovely park.

Blood Indian Park

The park has two campgrounds, a picnic area, rodeo grounds, a buffalo rubbing stone, and a monument dedicated to the people who made this project possible. Trees have been planted in long rows but are not yet tall enough to offer much shade. This park is like an oasis in the desert and is a welcome place to relax. Settle in for a few days of canoeing, sailing, swimming, or fishing for rainbow trout.

Hanna welcomes its visitors with a large model of the Canada grey goose at each end of town. The one at the east end is in a landing position while the other is taking off. Most of the businesses in Hanna have the bird painted on their signs or have a replica in their yard.

If you want to compare the jails of today with those of the past, see the Youngstown Jail at the Pioneer Museum. It is a cage about two metres (six feet) high, one metre (three feet) wide, and two metres (six feet) deep. The metal framework is in a grid pattern with openings of about

Youngstown Jail, Hanna

six centimetres (2.5 inches). The door is padlocked and a slot in the bottom allows for food to be passed to the prisoner.

The C.N.R. Roundhouse, built in 1912, is one of the few remaining in Canada. It is an important part of Alberta's history and really should be restored. Instead, it is being used as an auction market.

On the south side of the railroad tracks is the C.N. Reservoir, where you can cast for yellow perch. For rainbow trout, go two kilometres (1.2 miles) west of Hanna to the Helmer Reservoir.

CPR Roundhouse, Hanna

Eighteen kilometres (11 miles) south of Hanna on Highway #36 is the Sheerness Electrical Generating Station. Developed at a cost of approximately one billion dollars, it consumes about 150 hectares (370 acres) of coal each year. Near the plant is the Prairie Oasis Park, beside a pond covering over 480 hectares (1,200 acres). There is a campsite and the water is great for swimming, water skiing, and wind surfing.

Delia to Morrin

DELIA AND THE HAND HILLS

Because this was the Canadian National Railway's highest point between Calgary and Saskatoon, Delia was originally named Highland.

Turn south into Delia and follow #851 through the town to the Hand Hills. The road is paved through the hills, and from here you have a sweeping view of the prairie below. The Hand Hills have a fairly dense growth of trees as compared to the grassland around them. Mother's Mountain is the second highest elevation between the Rocky Mountains and Labrador. The Cypress Hills surpass it by a mere 4.5 metres (14.5 feet). A word to the amateur palaeontologist - some of the fossils found in these hills have come from elephants, camels, and horses.

ROWLEY

Back on Highway #9 continue west to Highway #56, then turn north. This rates as one of Alberta's most charming rural drives. If you have the time, drive all the way to Highway #13.

The hills and corresponding depressions along this road are known as knobs and kettles. These mound-like rises are so compacted together they look like giant skiing moguls. The farmhouses in the area have large, brightly-coloured yards and the fields are green or gold with crops. The blue waters of many ponds reflect the gray of dead tree trunks, the green of bordering trees, and the white of the clouds overhead.

Restored Rowley Trading Post

Rowley, also known as Rowleywood, is just 5.6 kilometres (3.5 miles) west of this highway and well worth a visit. The Museum of Yesteryear is in the railway station and across from the museum is Boxcar Park. The park has a miniature pool with a foot bridge, flowers, and benches for the weary. But that is not all there is in this hamlet — take a good look at their main street.

Some of the disused buildings have been repaired and furnished with a western theme. Sam's Saloon, with its bat wing doors, and the Rowley Trading Post are just two examples. They have hitching rails, wagon wheels, and benches in front. Inside are numerous reminders of the past, such as moonshine jugs, liquor bottles, period clothing, glassware, and baskets.

There are only about 14 residents in the town of Rowley, and it is the community spirit of these people and the surrounding district that made the street possible. And if the locale seems familiar, it probably is. The movie *Bye Bye Blues* was filmed here.

Bye Bye Blues

Bye Bye Blues was written and directed by Ann Wheeler and is set in the 1940s during the war. It is a story of woman, played by Rebecca Jenkins, who must support her children while her husband is overseas. She joins a band as a piano player and singer (Ms. Jenkins did all the singing herself). • The producers drove many miles throughout Alberta before finding Rowley, with its old main street. Shells were constructed over some of the existing buildings to make them appear to be from the 1940s and the grain elevators were even repainted to the 1940s colour of brown. • The project was filmed in Alberta and India in 1988-89 and cost $4.5 million.

MORRIN

Go back to Highway #9 and turn west for a quick visit to Morrin, "Where The Pioneer Spirit Lives." Near the town's welcome sign, you will find a threshing machine, a plow, a wagon, a covered wagon, an early tractor, and two buildings.

At the historical village in the town is a sod house, one of only two in Alberta. Constructed for the town's homecoming a few years ago, it contains many of the household items used during the days of the early settlers.

Sod Houses

Material for the construction of a frame or log home was not always available to the first settlers who arrived in Alberta. Being inventive, though, they utilized the resources available and built sod houses. They cut strips of sod about 0.5 by 1.2 metres (two by four feet) and overlapped them for the walls. Doors and windows were installed and wood or poles were laid to form the roof framework. They arranged more sod on these to form the roof. • Their home was warm in winter, cool in summer, and the roof turned a bright green as the grass grew. But there was one major drawback: when it rained, the roof soaked up the water and it drizzled inside the house for days after a storm.

Drumheller and District

Dinosaurs (terrible reptiles) roamed the earth between 65 and 225 million years ago, but it was not until 1824 that the first evidence of their existence was discovered in southern England. Since then, bones, teeth, and eggs have been found on all continents.

Badlands near Drumheller

Alberta's badlands may be sparse in vegetation, but they are rich in history. The first discovery of a prehistoric animal in Alberta was in 1884: a fossilized head was found near Drumheller in the centre of the badlands by Joseph B. Tyrrell, a geologist with the Geological Survey of Canada. Many full and partial skeletons have been collected since that initial unearthing.

Badlands

The main canyon of Alberta's badlands (land that is not arable or productive) varies from 62 to 154 metres (200 to 500 feet) deep and can reach a width of over 1.6 kilometres (one mile). Carved mainly by the Red Deer River, the badlands stretch through much of southern Alberta. Other winding courses through the badlands were dug by separate streams. • The steep bluffs, fluted gullies, and desert-like vegetation offer a strikingly unique beauty. The multi-coloured layers of the bluffs range from black to brown and gray to white and are comprised of coal, clay, ironstone, shale, and sandstone that were laid down during millions of years of changes in the earth's surface. Through erosion, these layers and the remains of the dinosaurs have been exposed.

DINOSAUR TRAIL

To see the effects of Mother Nature's work and many man-made sights, follow the Dinosaur Trail, a 48 kilometre (30 mile) circular route that begins and ends in Drumheller. As you descend into the badlands on Highway #9, watch for Secondary Highway #838. Turn west and you are on the Dinosaur Trail.

One-third of a kilometre along the trail, on the south side of the road, is the Homestead Museum, with over 4,000 catalogued items. Just a short distance further you enter Midland Provincial Park.

Royal Tyrrell Museum of Palaeontology

Camping is not permitted in the park, but McMullen Island offers quiet picnic areas set in tall, shady trees. There is good fishing, bird watching, and many hiking trails. Also in the park is the old Midland Mining Office and the Royal Tyrrell Museum of Palaeontology.

The Midland Mining Company produced coal for nearly 50 years until an international switch to natural gas and oil in the 1950s forced the mine to close in 1959. The mining office, on the north side of the road, was built in 1912. Inside are the original vault, the accountant's desk, and black and white photographs showing the mine in its heyday. Take one of the self-guiding trails leading from the office to the remains of some of the mine sites.

A short drive further along the trail brings you to the road to the Royal Tyrrell Museum of Palaeontology. The museum incorporates 11,200 square metres (120,600 square feet) of space, with 4,400 square metres (47,400 square feet) of display area. It is open year round and is popular with visitors from around the world.

Inside the museum are 16 separate sections where you can see the earth's history, perform some experiments of your own using computers, or see the evolution of life on the planet. You can also view a prehistoric garden with plants that flourished during the dinosaurs' reign, some species of which are still thriving today.

Other exhibits include the remains of flying reptiles and marine invertebrates, the ice age, the age of reptiles, and over thirty complete dinosaurs. At the main lab, a large window allows you to watch dinosaur speci-

Hoodoos near Drumheller

mens being prepared. Tours are available and donations are gratefully accepted.

Outside, a set of steps leads to a look-out from which you can scan this barren region. Many hiking trails diverge from the museum through hills on the eight hectare (20 acre) site. Remember, though, that you cannot keep any specimens or fossils you might find.

Royal Tyrrell Museum of Palaeontology

The Royal Tyrrell Museum of Palaeontology was opened on September 25, 1985. It was named after Joseph Burr Tyrrell, who discovered the dinosaur beds of the badlands, and is the only facility in Canada dedicated totally to dinosaur research. While most of its specimens come from Alberta's badlands, some are also from other parts of the world. Members of the Tyrrell Museum staff have travelled to the Gobi Desert in China, to search for and study dinosaur skeletons.

From the museum, turn west back onto Highway #838, and within a short distance, you will reach the Chapel of Contemplation, also known as the Little Church. Built in 1957, it was designed to "seat 30,000 people, six at a time." Duck your head and enter through the small doorway, and don't forget to sign the guest book.

As the Dinosaur Trail begins to climb out of the valley, you will arrive at Horse Thief Canyon. A sign explains how the canyon received its name:

Horsethief Canyon

"In the early days ranching was the important industry in this area. Thousands of horses ranged from here to beyond the Hand Hills. Legend has it that horses would disappear into these canyons of the Red Deer River. Later they reappeared carrying a different brand. Hence the name... Horse Thief Canyon."

For an alternate view, take one of the paths down into the canyon and do some exploring. In wet weather, the slopes can be very slippery.

If you continue along the trail a few more miles you will reach the Bleriot Ferry and the halfway point of your journey. This ferry is one of only a handful of cable ferries operating in Alberta. It will transport any size of vehicle across the Red Deer River and is open from 7 a.m. to 11 p.m., April to November.

On the second half of your tour, you can drive to the Orknay Hill Viewpoint for another look at the badlands. At the Dry Canyon Trading Post and Petting Zoo, children can let off some of their energy at the playground or on the trampoline. While the

Bleriot Ferry

kids enjoy themselves, adults can browse through the trading post situated in an old cabin.

On the last part of the Dinosaur Trail, you will pass by the village of Nacmine, which is spread out between the Red Deer River and the road. There are three mine sites, the Red Deer Mine, the Commander Mine, and the Newcastle Mine, on the road back to Drumheller.

East Coulee Drive and Wayne Drive

On Highway #10, you will pass through a few small communities that once were large towns during the coal mining days. Market gardens are found throughout the area and you can buy fruits and vegetables in season.

If you like bridge crossings, take Highway #10X from Rosedale to the mining town of Wayne. The highway has been noted in Ripley's *Believe It Or Not* because of the nine bridges over the Rosebud River in the four mile drive to Wayne and the two more just past the turn to the town. All the bridges are one lane, so you have to yield to oncoming traffic. The spans are different sizes, colours, and styles.

Watch for the many historic signs along the road describing the mining history of Wayne. If you have worked up a thirst after crossing all those bridges, stop at the Last Chance Saloon in Wayne for refreshments and a taste of the past. Order a beer and it will be served in a quart sealer.

Rosedale Suspension Bridge

Head back to Rosedale and the Rosedale Suspension Bridge, a footbridge once used by miners to cross the Red Deer River on their way to work at the Star Mine.

When the Star Mine first opened in 1912, the miners used a rowboat to cross the river, then in 1919, a cable car system was built to convey both miners and coal. In 1931, the original swinging bridge was constructed and the miners had to brave strong winds and floods to reach the pit. The Star Mine closed in 1957, and the swinging bridge was rebuilt in 1958 as a reminder of the area's mining history.

One hundred and sixteen metres (380 feet) long, the bridge sways and bounces a little as people cross. But it is very exciting to look down at the river rushing below your feet.

Continue south on #10 to the hoodoos, the trademark of the badlands. Stone "caps" on the hoodoos have protected them from the wind and water that have eroded the sandstone around them. They are very fragile and a sign asks visitors not to climb on them. Judging by the number of people clambering over them to have their pictures taken, it appears that very few can read. Across the highway is a parking lot and picnic area.

Church at Dorothy

If you want to see a ghost town, turn east on #573 towards Dorothy and Little Fish Lake Provincial Park. Follow the road to the sign for Dorothy and take the short drive into the townsite. There are a few houses still occupied, some ramshackle buildings, and a campsite. Two dilapidated churches face each other against the backdrop of the hills. This once prosperous town in the Red Deer valley badlands offers some beautiful scenery.

Little Fish Lake is a bright blue colour and is shallow for a great distance from shore. Rows of planted trees shade the camping sites and there is a playground and a tap for water.

East Coulee is the terminus of Highway #10. It is a small town whose 1930s school is now a provincial historic site. Inside is a museum with a restored school room and coal mining room, a tea room, an art gallery, and a craft store.

Drive through the town to the wooden train trestle/vehicle bridge where the tracks run down the centre of one lane. It is closed to traffic but you are able to walk across. Erected in 1936, it is the only dual purpose bridge left standing in Western Canada.

Tipple at Atlas Coal Mine Museum

A gravel road leads from East Coulee to the Atlas Coal Mine Museum. It is also a provincially designated historic site and has Canada's last standing ore-sorting tipple of its type. (A tipple is a building where mining carts are emptied by tipping.) Tours are available for a small charge and donations to help restore the tipple are welcome.

DRUMHELLER

There is much to see in Drumheller: the Fossil Shop, where you can buy fossil jewellery; Tyrannosaurus Rex, a giant dinosaur at the bridge over the Red Deer River; Prehistoric Park and Ollie's Rock and Fossil Shop, where life size dinosaurs roam in the canyon scenery; the Buffalo Paddock; the Drumheller Dinosaur and Fossil Museum; and Reptile World, with Canada's largest live reptile display. Your children will be pleased to know that they can purchase a pet from Reptile World, complete with cage and supplies.

Horseshoe Canyon

There are three campgrounds in Drumheller for those who want to spend a few days seeing the sites. If you want to fish while visiting the badlands, the Red Deer River has walleye, pike, and goldeye.

Take Highway #9 west from Drumheller to the Horseshoe Canyon where, once again, the haunting badlands scenery spreads out before you. This canyon is most spectacular when the setting sun turns the slopes a reddish-gold colour. You can walk down into the canyon, but only if the trails are dry. Buy an authentic fossil as a souvenir from the owners of the van at the parking lot.

Rosebud to Dry Island Buffalo Jump

ROSEBUD

For a change of pace, continue west on Highway #9 until you reach Highway #840 to Rosebud. An art gallery, operated by the Rosebud Fellowship, is housed in the old United Church and the fellowship also operates the Rosebud School of the Arts and the Rosebud Dinner Theatre. The school and dinner theatre are located in the old mercantile store, first opened in 1911.

Three plays of six weeks duration each are presented at the theatre in the spring, the summer, and the fall. Dinner is served at 6 p.m. and the stage show begins at 8 p.m. Reservations are required.

Also in Rosebud are the Centennial Museum in the old Chinese Laundry and a honey processing plant. The museum is open during the theatre runs and you are able to tour the processing plant and buy fresh honey from the owners.

Continue west on Highway #9 to Highway #21 and turn north. Stop in at Fyten Reservoir, two kilometres (1.2 miles) south of Swalwell, and try for rainbow trout. If your luck is poor there,

Braconnier's Reservoir, 4.3 kilometres (2.6 miles) south of Three Hills, is also stocked with this fish.

Three Hills

Three Hills was named for the trio of hills five kilometres (three miles) north of the town. It is the home of the Prairie Bible Institute which draws students from all over Canada and the world for training in the mission field. Doctors and nurses also pursue their studies here to become medical missionaries. The music department has a 250 voice choir and many concerts are held in the auditorium, one of the largest in Alberta. Visitors are always welcome to tour the institute.

Trochu

"Arboretum — a place where trees and shrubs, especially rare ones, are grown and exhibited for scientific, educational, and other purposes."

The arboretum in Trochu is such a location. A red rock path takes you through the more than 1,000 trees and shrubs of 100 different species. The trees, many not native to the prairies, were planted between the 1920s and the 1950s. Most of the plants have explanatory signs in front of them. If you get tired, rest on one of the benches or relax in the gazebo set in the cool shade. Plan to spend an afternoon in the serene beauty of the Trochu Arboretum.

Dry Island Buffalo Jump Provincial Park

For one last look at the rugged, fascinating badlands, take the road to Dry Island Buffalo Jump Provincial Park, about 14 kilometres (8.5 miles) north of Trochu. The terrain appears flat for many kilometres, with cattle grazing contentedly in the fields. Suddenly, you are on the edge of a deep chasm with the Red Deer River flowing far below.

If you wish to go down to the day use area by the river, drive slowly. The road is very steep and winding, with several hairpin curves. Leave your trailer at the top. A row of trees separates the picnic site from the river bank and you can walk along a deer path to the water. You will have to put your vehicle in first or second gear for the trip out of the valley, and beware of the drive in wet weather.

Dry Island Buffalo Jump Provincial Park.

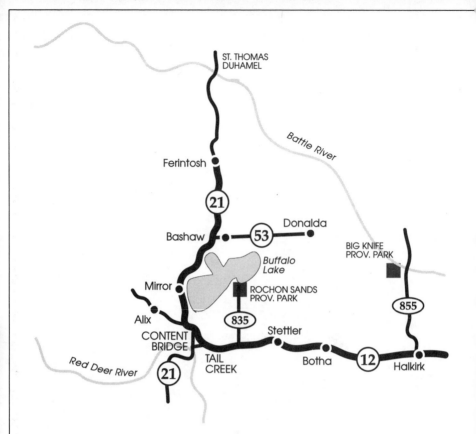

Chapter 6

Consort to Ferintosh

The Canadian Pacific Railway built its line through this region of Alberta in 1911. As was their custom, they sometimes bypassed existing hamlets and established their own townships along the track. Since 1911 was also the year George V was crowned King of England, several of the newly created communities were named in honour of the event. Can you guess which ones they were?

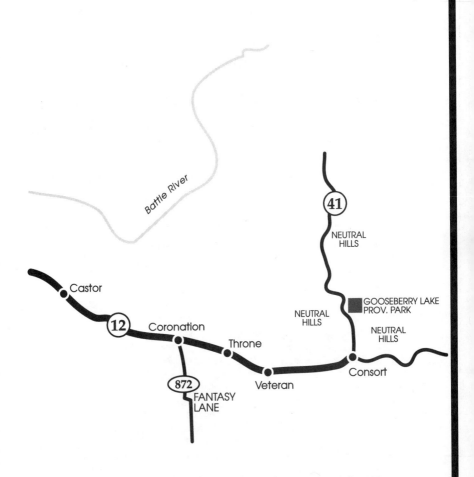

North of Veteran are the Nose Hills, a group of soft rolling hills covered in green grass and formed in the shape of a nose. Because of the bones discovered at the base of one of the hills (Buffalo Fall), the hills are believed to have been the site of a buffalo jump at one time. Climb to the top for a broad view of Alberta's parkland. The prettiest time to visit is in the spring, when the hills are covered by a mass of purple crocuses.

Consort to Botha

According to Native legend, the Great Spirit raised the Neutral Hills, north of Consort, to prevent two hostile tribes from meeting. The tribes, heeding the sign, decided to make peace and celebrated the occasion with a great feast.

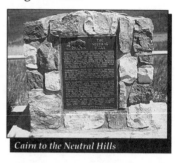

Cairn to the Neutral Hills

Natives roamed the hills for centuries and left behind teepee rings, cairns, and boulder outline effigies as evidence of their presence. The tourist information booth has a map indicating the location of many of these, but it isn't very specific. Some remains are a mile or two off the road and since there are no signs, they are difficult to find. If you really want to see some of these cultural features, ask at the information booth about a guided tour.

k. d. lang

k. d. (Kathryn Dawn) lang was born in Wetaskiwin in 1961 but moved with her family to the Consort area when she was about 18 months old. She grew up with a love for music and took piano and guitar lessons as a child. She began her professional singing career in Edmonton in 1983. • In the years since, she has sung with many great country and western stars, including the late Roy Orbison, and has won numerous Juno Awards and two Grammy Awards for her music. In the fall of 1990, the Canadian Academy of Recording Arts and Sciences presented k. d. with the Artist of the Decade (1981 to 1991) award. • She has toured North America and Europe and has branched out into movies, filming *Salmonberries* in Alaska in 1990.

Gooseberry Provincial Park is also in the Neutral Hills. Stay at one of the many campsites and spend your time swimming, waterskiing, boating, or fishing. Enjoy a round of golf on the free 9-hole course.

As you drive between Consort and Halkirk you will see countless green and brown birdhouses nailed to fence posts. These houses were erected to keep the mountain bluebird, a native to the prairie, parklands, and mountains, from disappearing. Much of its natural habitat has been destroyed by farming, and the more

Mountain bluebird

aggressive English sparrow and European starling have dominated the mountain bluebird's habitat. Now, with about one-third of the houses occupied by this beautiful sky-blue coloured bird, its continued presence is assured.

VETERAN AND THRONE

Continue west to Veteran, the home of the Veteran Eagle. Constructed by four men from the town in 1932, the Eagle was a two passenger Pietenpol monoplane with a wing span of 8.6 metres (28 feet) and weighing 309 kilograms (680 pounds). The craft could fly at 113 kilometres (70 miles) per hour and was occasionally used to deliver the weekly newspaper.

North of Veteran are the Nose Hills, a group of soft rolling hills covered in green grass and formed in the shape of a nose. Because of the bones discovered at the base of one of the hills (Buffalo Fall), the hills are believed to have been the site of a buffalo jump at one time. Climb to the top for a broad view of Alberta's parkland. The prettiest time to visit is in the spring, when the hills are covered by a mass of purple crocuses.

As you near Throne, watch for an ostrich family across the highway from the Throne Store. The birds came from Invermere, B.C. and cost about $12,000 each. Their value jumped to between $40,000 and $60,000 when they produced fertilized eggs.

If you want to get a closer look at the ostriches, drive slowly into the farm yard so as not to scare them and ask at the house. Don't get too close, because the curious birds will peck at anything bright and shiny you might be wearing. Also, when on the defensive, they will kick forward with lightning speed. While you are there, ask if there are any chicks.

CORONATION

Continue along Highway #12 to Coronation. North of the ball diamonds is a campsite and Coronation Pond. The fishing pond was developed by the Coronation Elks Lodge, the Coronation Lions, the Town of Coronation, and the Alberta Fish and Wildlife Division. Stocked with trout by Fish and Wildlife, it is a good place for fishing, canoeing, and sailing. Power boats are prohibited. A buffalo rubbing stone, a dedication to the early pioneers and a commemoration of Alberta's 75th anniversary, can be found in the park.

Buffalo Rubbing Stone, Coronation

Ogopogo's Pond, Fantasy Lane

If you are in the area in the fall, stop into Christie's of Coronation, on Windsor Avenue, and see the long tables of poinsettias. Christine Wagner grows her plants from cuttings and sells about 15,000 each fall.

For a totally unique experience, travel 4.3 kilometres (2.6 miles) down Highway #872 south of Coronation to Fantasy Lane. The lane, 3.2 kilometres (two miles) in length, is composed of a number of scenes laid out on private land along the highway. These are subject to change each year.

One, on the west side of the road, is called Nessie's Lair. The elusive Loch Ness Monster makes a special appearance in this small body of water. Standing on a rock beside the pond is the figure of a woman dressed in a kilt.

Nessie's Lair, Fantasy Lane

Districts of the Northwest Territories

The Hudson's Bay Company was granted a large segment of North America, comprising all the lands that drain into the Hudson's Bay, by King Charles II in 1670. The region was named Rupert's Land in honour of one of the King's cousins, who was the first governor of the company. • The new Dominion of Canada formed in 1867, and had purchased Rupert's Land from the Company by 1869. The new land, known as the North West Territories, was divided into four districts: Alberta, Athabasca, Saskatchewan, and Assiniboia. • Alberta was named after the daughter of Queen Victoria — Princess Louise Caroline Alberta — and is known as the Princess Province. The northern border of the new district lay between Athabasca Landing (Athabasca) and Slave Lake, the eastern boundary was just west of where St. Paul is today, the southern was at the U.S. border and the western boundary was formed by the Rocky Mountains.

Just down the road on the east side is Ogopogo Pond. The great beast of Lake Okanagan is slowly undulating towards an unsuspecting fisherman who is hoping to land a "big one."

Don't dash into Sasquatch Bluff—the "big guy" is hiding in the trees. If snakes bother you, stay away from Snakeville, where giant vipers slither about in the field.

Sasquatch Bluff, Fantasy Lane

Fisherman's Rock is the last on the lane. A large family has set up camp at the dugout and father is firmly anchored on top of a giant rock, trying to catch a fish for the evening meal.

Carry on south, past Fantasy Lane, until the highway curves to the east. Take the first gravel road east and follow it about one kilometre to a fenced area on the north side of the road. Within the fence is the cairn marking the meeting place of the districts of Alberta, Assiniboia, and Saskatchewan, three of the four provincial districts formed by the federal government in 1882.

CASTOR

As you near Castor, watch for the tall, sandstone bluffs along the bright, blue Castor Creek. If you take a quiet, scenic canoe trip down the creek, expect to see wildlife along the banks.

Fifteen kilometres (nine miles) south of Castor on Highway #36 and four kilometres (2.5 miles) east is Glenn's Game Farm. The farm has miniature horses, llama rides for children, and a variety of exotic animals and birds including Guinea fowl, peacocks, yaks, and buffalo.

Castor Creek, near Castor

The Huber Dam, with its trout-stocked reservoir, is east of Castor on Secondary Highway #599. On the Battle River north of Castor is the Valley Ski Hill, complete with six runs, a ski school, a day lodge, and a rental shop.

Horticulturists will want to continue further east on #599 to two flower greenhouses.

Evergreen Greenhouse was constructed by Ken and Rita James in 1989, and in the winter of 1990, they planted 5,200 plants from California. They now have seven varieties of roses and sell directly to flower shops. If you wish to see the roses call ahead to (403) 882-2161 for directions.

Thieleman Greenhouse was built in 1990 and houses Asiatic and Oriental lilies. Call (403) 882-2546 for directions so you may stop in and have your bouquet hand picked for you.

Sulphate

In the vicinity of a triangle formed by Castor, Oyen on Highway #9, and Provost on #13, there are many bodies of water containing a high amount of saline. As the water evaporates, it leaves the ground white with salt. This explains why you will see lakes or ponds with a white shore and numerous blocks of white, cracked, low ground in this section of Alberta. • South of Metiskow, which is west of Provost, is an Agassiz Resources mineral plant on the lake shore. This plant processes over 180 metric tons (200 tons) of sodium sulphate each day. •Around part of the lake is white berm constructed of salt. The white is so bright it hurts your eyes if you look at it too long.

Eleven kilometres (6.8 miles) north of Halkirk on Highway #855 you will find a gravel thoroughfare heading east. Turn down it and you will arrive right in the middle of badlands similar to those at Drumheller. The hills are brown, red, and white with different shades in between.

Badlands north of Halkirk

Botha, just east of Stettler, is the home of Canada's first flying machine and the country's first manned flight, which occurred here on August 10, 1907. Three Underwood brothers designed and built a 205 kilogram (450 pound) eight by 13 metre (26 by 42 foot) oval wing with controls, a propeller, and a platform for the engine and pilot. The machine was intended to soar under its own power, but their inability to obtain a suitable engine prevented it from doing so.

In an effort to fly, the Underwoods tied the craft to the ground with a long rope and allowed the wind to raise it into the air with one of the brothers aboard. They attached lanterns to the wing when they "flew" at night. They also constructed what was probably Canada's first airstrip, a 405 metre (1,320 foot) long runway for the machine. As you drive past the hamlet, watch for the huge mural of the flying wing on the wall of the Botha arena on the north side of the highway.

Mural of the Undrwood's flying wing, Botha Arena

Stettler to Duhamel

Would you like to take a nostalgic ride on a steam-powered train? Then contact Alberta Prairie Steam Tours in Stettler at 1-800-282-3994. The train leaves Stettler and steams to various communities between Camrose and Drumheller. The excursion times vary between four and ten hours, depending on whether you wish to be entertained at a barbeque or corn roast at one of the many villages and towns along the route.

The Stettler Town and Country Museum is located on 3.2 hectares (eight acres) in the southwest corner of town. It has many displays and several dated buildings, including the large two storey courthouse which was built in 1906-07 and the Ransom School, built in 1905.

Steam engine, Stettler

One of the main attractions of the museum is the Dutch Windmill, assembled by the Dutch Society to salute the men who fought and died for the freedom of Holland in the Second World War.

TAIL CREEK

Tail Creek is a small stream that drains Buffalo Lake into the Red Deer River. The town of Tail Creek, during its short life (1870 to 1880), was the largest settlement at the time in the West. It had more than 2,000 inhabitants and 400 log cabins, at a time when St. Boniface had a population of 750 and Winnipeg only 250.

Each fall, its citizenry swelled as Métis and Natives from other parts of the province arrived for the great buffalo hunt. For a few years, a four-member NWMP force was stationed at the town to keep an eye on the residents and to apprehend whiskey traders from the south.

Just as the Métis depended on the buffalo, so did the town. As the herds were quickly depleted in the late 1870s, the town, too, quickly died. A fire burned through the community leaving one structure standing. No one bothered to rebuild the town and the sole surviving building was later moved to Stettler. Now, all that is left of Tail Creek is the old cemetery.

Tail Creek Cemetery

To find the graveyard, go north from Content Bridge on Highway #21 until you come to a plant on the west side of the highway. Turn east on the road towards Stettler and travel until you see the Tail Creek Cemetery Road sign. Turn south and drive two kilometres (1.2 miles) to the cemetery.

The grounds are overrun by weeds and you will have to walk to the rear of the yard to discover traces of the graves. Some have headstones which are broken or have fallen over, while others are identified by unmarked crosses or posts. A cairn, dedicated to the Métis who initiated the town, is in the southeast corner.

ALIX

Alix is on Highway #12, just west of #21. There are many artifacts from Tail Creek at the Wagon Wheel Museum. On the right side of the street leading to the campsite in Alix is a small park where you will find two red brick flower boxes. On the second planter is a plaque to Mary Irene Parlby, one of "The Group of Five" who led the women's equal rights movement of the early 1900s.

Buffalo Lake is for pike fishermen, but if trout is what you are looking for, try the Mirror Reservoir, one kilometre (0.6 miles) west of Alix. No motorized craft are allowed on the reservoir but don't let that stop you. Rainbows up to about 2.3 kilograms (five pounds) have been hooked.

BASHAW AND DONALDA

Bashaw bills itself "Cheese Capital of Western Canada" because it is the home of Armstrong Cheese, the largest cheese producer in western Canada, and Northern Alberta Dairy Pool, another cheese manufacturer. You are welcome to enter either outlet and buy some of their cheeses over the counter.

Turn east at Bashaw onto Highway #53 and take the 28 kilometre (17 mile) drive to Donalda, Canada's Lamp Capital, to visit the Donalda Lamp Museum. Inside is a unique collection of over 700 kerosene lamps, most of which were donated by families in the community. Many of these light vessels are from the 1800s. A carbide bicycle lamp, an Aladdin's lamp, a coal oil bicycle lamp, and kerosene lamps are on display.

During the Victorian era, lamps in the parlours of families with young girls contained only enough fuel for a short visit from a suitor.

Other exhibits in the museum include old washboards, spinning wheels, outdated tools, and over 350 pairs of salt and pepper shakers. If you have any memorabilia you would like to display, contact the museum, since exhibits are changed often.

The museum stands above Meeting Creek Coulee, and Donalda Coulee is less than one kilometre east of the town. Both have intriguing rock patterns and you might want to hike through them with a camera or an easel.

A few other attractions in the area are the Shorthills Trout Pond, three kilometres (1.9 miles) west of Donalda, and the Willow Canyon Ski Hill, which offers downhill and cross-country skiing, just north of town. The Donalda Co-operative Creamery is one of two independent creameries remaining in Alberta.

North of Bashaw is the town of Ferintosh, where you can buy sausage to combine with your Armstrong cheese for lunch. King Kuby Sausage is a small, family run business that prepares ham sausage, smoked bratwurst, pepperoni, smokies, garlic sausage, beef jerky, Kuby burgers, and ready-to-cook pizzas. Just follow the signs in town.

DUHAMEL

North of Ferintosh is the Duhamel campsite on the Battle River. Here you can eat your cheese and sausage at one of the picnic tables, then try some fishing in the river for pickerel and perch. Or you can learn a little history.

South of the driveway into the campsite is a cairn dedicated to old Duhamel (1878-1910) and two historic signs describing the Grand Trunk Pacific Railway and the Laboucane Settlement.

The area along the Battle River was settled by a party of Métis buffalo hunters and their families in the 1870s. The colony was originally named Laboucane Settlement after two brothers but in 1881, a mission was established and the name was changed to St. Thomas Duhamel.

St. Thomas Catholic Church, Duhamel

From the campsite, follow the winding gravel road south and watch for a painting of a train crossing a high, wooden bridge. As the Grand Trunk Pacific Railway went through here, it crossed the valley on a bridge 40 metres (120 feet) above the Battle River.

Cross the railway tracks to a faded "Historical Site" marker and take the road running to St. Thomas Church. Partially hidden by a row of trees on the south side, St. Thomas Catholic Church was open from 1883 to 1962 and has been preserved by the Duhamel Historical Society.

The villages named for the coronation of King George V are Consort, Veteran, Throne, and Coronation. Three other communities, Loyalist, Federal, and Fleet, were designated at the same time but have since disappeared.

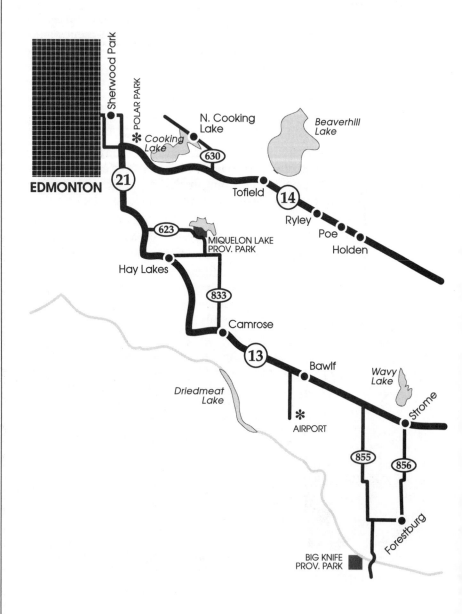

Chapter 7
Hardisty to Wainwright

This circuit is completely within Alberta's aspen parkland zone. You can expect to see some beautiful landscape, especially as you drive through the hills along the Battle River.

The Iron Creek Meteorite, the largest meteorite found to date in Canada, was discovered northeast of Killam by Reverend George McDougall in 1869. The meteorite is about 1,000 years old and weighs 165 kilograms (363 ponds). It was delivered to a museum in Toronto shortly after its discovery, but is now in the Provincial Museum of Alberta in Edmonton.

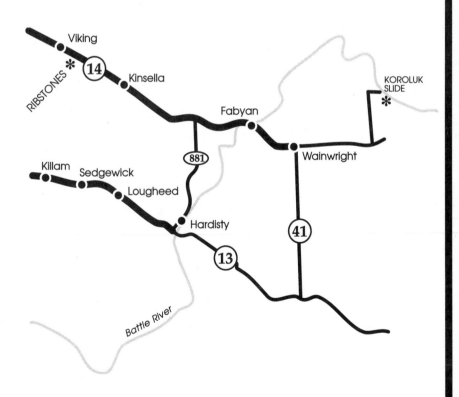

Hardisty to Bawlf

HARDISTY

Hardisty is known as "Flag Capital of The World." A Flag Society was formed in the town a few years ago, and it received hundreds of banners and many messages from world leaders that encouraged tolerance, understanding, and brotherhood throughout the world. The flags hung in various sections of town until the society disbanded.

Flags at Hardisty Rodeo Grounds

Now, the only time you will see these flags flying is during the Hardisty Rodeo, when they are positioned around the rodeo grounds. Some of them are also on display at the Town office. At the Park of Provinces, you can see flags from across Canada and read the messages from the Prime Minister, the provincial premiers, and the territorial administrators.

During the rodeo, stay at the Hardisty Lake Park across from the grounds. The lake is a lovely blue and great for waterskiing, swimming, and boating. Fishermen will be pleased to know it is stocked with trout.

In the fall, hunters might want to try for whitetail and mule deer in the area.

LOUGHEED, SEDGEWICK, AND KILLAM

Lougheed was named after Senator Sir James Lougheed, former Premier Peter Lougheed's grandfather. For a look at the shoemaker's trade, visit the Iron Creek Museum in the village. You will see stitching machines, tools, old shoes, and samples of leather used by the shoemaker of a by-gone era.

Sedgewick won second prize in a "Best Water in Western Canada" competition. Their water source is only 5.5 metres (18 feet) below ground level.

The Iron Creek Meteorite, the largest meteorite found to date in Canada, was discovered northeast of Killam by Reverend George McDougall in 1869. The meteorite is about 1,000 years old and weighs 165 kilograms (363 pounds). It was delivered to a museum in Toronto shortly after its discovery, but is now in the Provincial Museum of Alberta in Edmonton.

The Sterling Flour Mills were constructed in Strome in 1911 and, over the years, gained a reputation for their modern equipment, model facilities, and superior quality products. Flour from here was shipped to central and northern Alberta and Saskatchewan. Flour was in great demand during the First World War, but the need decreased after the war and the mill closed in 1920. Twelve years later, it reopened and ran on a limited basis until 1942, when production was increased due to the Second World War. After years of operating at partial capacity, it finally shut its doors in 1963.

The faded white buildings still stand in Strome and the machinery inside is in good condition. Maybe one day the site will be restored to show visitors how a flour mill operated.

Quicksilver Manufacturing is located in Strome. They fabricate fibreglass canoes and export them throughout North America. Take a tour of the plant and have a cup of coffee, on the company.

North of Strome is Wavy Lake, a favorite layover for geese and ducks on their migrations.

FORESTBURG

Forestburg is south of Strome on #856. In 1907, adventurous homesteaders from the area began developing drift mines, also known as "gopher hole" mines, in the seams of coal along the banks of the Battle River. The coal was extracted by hand and loaded into coal cars, which were hauled to the surface by hand or by horse power. As many as 25 mines operated in the area, and most of these were owned by local residents. The Bish brothers owned one of the largest and their 25 employees produced 8,000 tonnes (8,889 tons) annually.

Coal Mine Cart, Devonian Park, Forestburg

These underground mines produced coal until 1949, when the Sinclair Coal Company bought out the Battle River Syndicate, which had been formed by some of the coal owners. The name Forestburg Collieries was given to the operation, and surface mining was begun in the area in 1950. In 1956, the collieries were sold to the Luscar mining group.

In the Devonian Park, you will see a coal mine car, typical of those used in the underground mines in the area from 1905 to 1945. At the entrance to the park is a cairn to commemorate Forestburg's becoming a village in 1919. Also on the monument is a plaque to Anthony Henday who camped west of the village on Oct. 4, 1754 during his exploration of the West.

Anthony Henday

In 1754, Anthony Henday became the first European to enter what is now Alberta, north of where Chauvin is today. He was employed by the Hudson's Bay Company and his mission was to convince the Blackfoot to make the four month round trip voyage to the Hudson's Bay to trade their furs. • With his Cree guides, he journeyed west and camped for three days in the valley of the Battle River. Like the Cree, Henday travelled on foot. When he reached an Assiniboine camp near present-day Irma, he bartered a gun for a horse, and so became Alberta's first white horse trader. • Henday was used to the grimy, disordered state of Cree camps, and wasn't prepared for the grandeur of the Blackfoot encampment. Two hundred teepees were assembled in two rows almost a mile long, and the Chief's tent could accommodate 50 people. • After smoking grand-pipes and eating boiled buffalo meat, Henday made his proposal. The Blackfoot Chief turned down Henday's request, politely pointing out that it was a great distance and they were not paddlers. Undaunted, Henday tried again the next day. Once more, his suggestion was rejected. • Henday and his Cree companions left the Blackfoot and, travelling west, crossed the Red Deer River near Innisfail, where Henday became the first European to view the Rocky Mountains. They camped for the winter along the North Saskatchewan River near the mouth of the Sturgeon River, north of present-day Edmonton. • Henday and the Cree returned to York Factory on Hudson's Bay with 60 canoes laden with Blackfoot furs. The Blackfoot had actually been trading their furs to the Cree, who had claimed them as their own when they reached the Bay. Not wanting to waste their time travelling to trade furs, the Blackfoot had refused to change their lifestyle.

The scenery along the Battle River valley at Big Knife Provincial Park, nine kilometres (5.5 miles) south of Forestburg on #855, is superb. To take some great photographs of the many channels the river has cut, climb the hill on the north side of the roadway into the park. Be careful where you step — the hill is covered with bright-yellow-flowered, prickly pear cacti.

Big Knife Provincial Park

Forestburg Collieries at Paintearth Mine is twenty kilometres (12 miles) south of Forestburg on Highway #856 and one kilometre (0.6 miles) east on #601. Drive slowly along #601 and read the signs posted in the fields. These explain what was mined out, when the land was levelled, the date the soil was replaced, and when and what was seeded. Stop in at the office, Monday to Friday during office hours, for a tour or phone (403) 582-4112 for information.

BAWLF

The Lutheran Church in Bawlf is the third one to be constructed in the village. When the first one was destroyed by fire, the members of the congregation built a second one. When it, too, burned, they erected this last one: made of brick.

Alberta's Littlest Airport is four kilometres (2.5 miles) west of Bawlf and four kilometres south on Kelsey Road. The airport is located in a farmer's field, and various groups use it for weiner roasts, corn roasts, and fun days. Avid remote control pilots gather in the evenings to practice on the five runways for the owner-sponsored flying competition in August.

Camrose to Tofield

CAMROSE

Camrose is a very easy town to explore. Obtain a map at the Chamber of Commerce and begin your visit. As you near the vicinity of an attraction, watch for "City tour" street signs with an arrow and number. Industrial tours through the Stelco Pipe Mills and the Byers Flour Mill, home of Sunny Boy Cereals, are also available.

Rosehaven and the Camrose Museum are both on 53rd Street, between 46th and 47th Avenues. Constructed in 1912, the

Miquelon Lake Provincial Park

building housing Rosehaven was initially called the Camrose Normal School. It was the second school opened in Alberta for the education of teachers. When the University of Alberta began offering classes for would-be instructors, this school suspended operation. A new wing was added, the grounds were landscaped, and now it is a hospital called Rosehaven.

Camrose Lutheran College is renowned for its Viking Cup hockey tournament, which attracts teams from Canada, the United States, and Europe. The college is also a Nordic skiing training centre. One of Canada's oldest ski clubs is in Camrose, and the runs are used by skiers hoping to qualify for provincial and national championships.

If you happen to be in town during the first weekend in June, you can take part in the annual Jaywalkers Jamboree, which features the Great Canadian Chili Cook-Off.

The Camrose Golf course is in Victoria Park, in the northwest corner of town. About two kilometres (1.2 miles) north of Camrose, on #833, is the Whistle Stop Driving Range and Miniature Golf Course.

There are northern pike in Dried Meat Lake to the south of town, and each winter an ice fishing derby is held at the lake.

For those looking for a place to camp for the night, continue north on #833 to Miquelon Lake

Miquelon Lake Provincial Park

Provincial Park. It has 286 camping sites and long, wide, sandy beaches on a large lake. The warm water is great for swimming, sailing, boating, windsurfing, and waterskiing. There is a 9-hole golf course, a petting zoo, go-karts, and mini-golf at Miquelon Funland. You should be able to find something to do, unless you are a fisherman — no angling is allowed.

HAY LAKES

Hay Lakes is Southwest of Miquelon, on Highway #617, and just east of the town is a campground. Walk through the gate at the south end and follow the road to a large open field. There is a slight hill in the centre of the field with a monument and three flag poles. This is the site of the most westerly telegraph station on the Battleford line, established in 1877. However, the station only operated two years. When the telegraph was extended from Battleford to Fort Edmonton in 1879, this office was abandoned.

Telegraph

When Canada acquired the Northwest Territories from the Hudson's Bay Company in 1869, there was a desperate need for a communication system. Finally, in 1874, the federal government employed private contractors to build an electric telegraph line along a proposed Canadian Pacific Railway route. The line was put up between 1874-78 and ran between Fort William, north of Winnipeg, and Hay Lakes. This united Eastern Canada with the West. • There were numerous complaints about the length of time it took for messages to reach the population of the NWT. There were many reasons for slow service: inadequate poles that were sometimes held up by the wire; occasional sections were supported by tree limbs; poor maintenance of the line; undersized poles; green wooden brackets that dried and eventually fell off; insufficient slack for contraction during cold weather; prairie fires; and lightning strikes. • In 1879, the line was rerouted from Battleford, through Victoria Settlement and Fort Saskatchewan, to Fort Edmonton. At this time, the CPR boasted that it had the longest telegraph line, working on a continuous circuit, in North America.

COOKING LAKE

The Cooking Lake-Blackfoot Recreation, Wildlife, and Grazing Area is west of Sherwood Park and south of Elk Island National Park. One of the earliest steps in conservation occurred here in 1899, when Canada's first forest reserve, the Cooking Lake Forest Reserve, was established. Management of the holding was taken over by the Alberta government in 1930.

In 1948, local cattlemen organized the Blackfoot Grazing Association and leased the reserve for pasture. By the late 1970s, outdoor recreationists were using the sanctuary for their own pursuits. All these activities, along with natural gas production, created a problem. So, in order to look after the needs of the wildlife, cattle, gas producers, and humans, the Cooking Lake-Blackfoot Grazing, Wildlife and Provincial Recreation Area was launched. It is unequaled anywhere in Alberta.

The area is on 97 square kilometres (37 square miles) of wetlands, pastures, and forests. It is an island of wildlife in a sea of agricultural land. Coyote, elk, moose, and more than 200 varieties of birds occupy the reserve, along with the cattle.

There are four staging sites: two can be reached from Highway #14, one from Highway #16, and one from Range Road #210. Drive into the staging enclosure, park your vehicle, and you are free to hike, ride horses, cross country ski, snowshoe, and snowmobile. Enjoy yourself, but remember to respect the other users of the land.

POLAR PARK

Polar Park is the first park of its kind in Alberta. Its main purpose is to preserve and breed animals, many of which are endangered, from the colder climates of the world. As you pull into the parking lot, watch for a flock of Canada geese that circles the lot, lands, waddles around honking, then flies up and starts the procedure over again. When you climb out of your car, listen for the lonesome howl of the wolves. It will send a tingle down your spine.

Polar Park

The animals are kept outdoors, so the park is open year round. There are about 600 hectares (1,500 acres) of land in the sanctuary, and wide paths lead you to the various sections. The best time to view the animals is during their noon feeding, when they gather close to the fence. In the winter, there are more than 16 kilometres (10 miles) of cross-country ski trails which will take you through the park and out into the forest preserve.

TOFIELD

On the way to Tofield, watch for Highway #833. Go south for 9.6 kilometres (6 miles), then east for two kilometres (1.25 miles) to Knothole Woodcraft. There you will see some original wood products hand-crafted by Eva Loranger. Jewellery boxes, made from the end pieces of fence posts, and wood carvings line shelves. Wood-burning drawings and barbed wire plaques hang on the walls. Lamps with wooden bases, carved animals, and painted signs are just a few of her other creations.

Eva will take the time to visit with you. She will explain the various types of wood and how each gives a piece of work a distinct look. Much of the wood she uses — mesquite, oak, cedar, and pine — is collected on expeditions to the United States. She also buys wire at barbed wire shows in the States.

At Tofield, along the service road beside Highway #14, is the Tofield Nature Centre and an information booth. At the nature centre is a large collection of bird houses donated by various towns, businesses, and clubs throughout the area. Each one is different and has the name of the donor on it.

East of Tofield, on Highway #626 is the Beaverhill Lake Natural Area and Bird Sanctuary. The natural area was established to conserve and maintain the wildlife and wilderness around the lake.

A group of birding enthusiasts formed the Beaverhill Lake Bird Banding Station in 1983 to facilitate research on the birds of the lake and to provide training in field ornithology. The association was renamed the Beaverhill Bird Observatory in 1985 and has remained active in many projects.

Beaverhill Lake is one of two nationally sanctioned nature viewpoints, and is western Canada's only shore bird reserve. Over 250 species of birds have been identified at the lake and many of them are rare or endangered.

If you would like to see large migrations, or maybe spot a rare bird, visit Beaverhill Lake. In March, local nesting pairs of Canada Geese appear and signal that spring has arrived. Soon many other species begin to appear: red-tail hawks, bald eagles, harriers, peregrine falcons, pectoral sandpipers, and marbled godwits. By May, the lake is alive with thousands of waterfowl. Some continue north; some stay and nest.

Soon the woods, fields, and marshes are full of songbirds. Some of the rarer birds — the black-billed cuckoo, the red phalarope, or the sharp-tailed sparrow — might be seen by watchful birders.

Marbled godwit

To reach the Beaverhill Bird Observatory, follow Highway #626 (Rowan's Route) east of town. About four kilometres (2.5 miles) farther is a side road that leads to Francis Point.

Continue past Francis Point for another four kilometres and turn north. There is a closed gate across the access; make sure you secure it after you have entered the field. Drive slowly; the path is two tracks wide and deep ruts occasionally cut across it.

At the end of the path is another gate. This one you cannot drive through. Park your vehicle here, open the gate or climb through the fence, and proceed on foot. The walk to the observatory is through tall foliage and low wetland on the western shore of Robert Lister (or A) Lake. Eventually the path heads west away from this lake and ends at the bird observatory on Beaverhill Lake.

The trail is long, so make sure you have good hiking shoes, plenty of mosquito repellent, and a sun hat. Don't forget your camera. Because of the distance and the "herds'" of mosquitoes, only ardent bird watchers will want to make this trip.

Ryley to Wainwright

RYLEY, POE, AND HOLDEN

The welcoming sign at Ryley states "Live the Life of Ryley."

Have you heard of the famous "Captain and Mrs. Compost"? Did you know they make their home in Ryley? They are two people who dress in costumes and enter in local parades as mascots for Canada's first community compost project.

The natural fertilizer venture was begun by the residents of Ryley and district and is endorsed by the Village Council and the Department of the Environment. All organic matter — potato peels, coffee grounds, grass cuttings, anything originally taken from the ground — can be composted.

The villagers deliver their organic matter to a compound near the town where it is stored and left to work. Then, as they need it, they return to pick up the fertilizer for their yards and gardens. Ninety-four per cent of the village participates in the project.

The hamlet of Poe was named after the famous master of detective and horror stories, Edgar Allan Poe.

Holden does not have a museum, but you are allowed to visit the Holy Ghost Ukrainian Catholic Church to see its kaleidoscopic interior.

VIKING

In 1914, gas was found in the area and Viking became the centre of the Viking Gas Field. Natural gas from this field has served Edmonton, Red Deer, and towns between since that initial find.

The Viking Meat Market and Processing Plant is the "Home of the Famous Viking Sausage." The sausage is long and slim, like a pepperoni, although lighter in colour and not as wrinkled. It has a mild taste. It is sometimes called a wiener and you can munch on it while you travel.

Ribstone near Viking

The town is also the "Home of the Sutters," a family that had six brothers who played in the NHL at the same time.

To see the Viking Ribstones, watch for an historical sign about 11 kilometres (seven miles) east of the town. Just past that sign is a road heading south. Follow it until you come to a "T" intersection. Turn east and then immediately south again. There isn't a sign announcing the ribstones. Watch for the red and white fence posts surrounding a slight hill on the west side of the road. Drive to the top and you will find the ribstones and a cairn.

The large stones have carvings similar to the ribs of a buffalo. Scientists believe they were worshiped by Natives for many centuries. They left gifts of tobacco, beads, or meat beside the ribstones in the hopes that it would bring them luck during their hunt. This custom was continued until the late 1800s. Because they are of historic value, please do not disturb them.

KINSELLA AND FABYAN

Kinsella has a large building, divided into three businesses, along the highway. One is the Kinsella Kountry Store, another is the Kinsella Kountry Kafe, and the third is the Kinsella Kountry Post Office. The first log cabin in this hamlet, built in 1903, is used as a small museum.

If you are an antique lover, stop in at Antiques by Herrod in Fabyan. Turn south into the hamlet and drive one block past the old church. It is on the east side of the road. The owner operated an antique shop in Scotland for many years before moving back to Alberta, and most of the articles come from that country.

WAINWRIGHT

Camp Wainwright is Canada's second largest military training facility and western Canada's main training base. During the war, over 1,000 German officers were interred at the camp. A P.O.W. tower, with artifacts, commemorates that time. If you ask at the gate to see the tower, you will only be allowed to drive

POW Tower, Camp Wainwright

up to it and take pictures. A tour of the inside can be arranged at the Wainwright tourist booth.

Beside the camp is a paddock containing a small herd of buffalo. A narrow road follows the fence and there are many turnouts, called "Buffalo Lookout Parking," which hold about three vehicles. The best time to see these huge animals is in the evening when they come out of the bush for water and salt.

Canada's largest falcon facility is in Wainwright. Endangered Peregrine falcons are raised here and released into the wild. To view the Peregrine Falcon Facility, you must book a tour at the tourist information booth, because the road to the complex is through Camp Wainwright.

Buffalo National Park

Before Camp Wainwright was established, the area was known as Buffalo National Park. The park was created in 1908 on 592 square kilometres (234 square miles), and buffalo, elk, and moose roamed throughout its forests. In 1941, the buffalo were transferred to Elk Island National Park and the Department of National Defence took over the land.

Petroleum Park is on the same grounds as the tourist information booth. One of the first wooden oil pumps used in the area is on display. There is also an exhibit explaining the history of the petroleum industry in Wainwright.

About 20 kilometres (12 miles) east of Wainwright, on Highway #14, is the turn to the Koroluk Slide. The route is gravel, and you will pass the United Church of Rosedale, built in 1933. Continue for 22 kilometres (13.6 miles), then turn east at the "T" and drive to the slide.

The Koroluk slide occurred in 1974 and was caused when the subsoil strata (the layer of earth just under the ground surface) became saturated with water and very slippery. The heavy topsoil squeezed the subsoil and the subsoil (still underneath the surface) slid down the slope until it found a spot where the topsoil was lighter. Some of the earth slid 230 metres (750 feet) before stopping.

While this was happening, the surface soil sank to replace the lost subsoil, some of it dropping 12 to 15 metres (40 to 50 feet). The crops, grass, and bushes growing on the topsoil were barely disturbed by the change in their location.

Walk through the gate into the field and take a look at the slide area and the fence hanging out over the fallen terrain. Be careful where you stand. Cracks are opening up in the ground close to the edge of the cliff.

Koroluk slide

Chapter 8
Devon to Crossfield

Highway #2 is a perfect example of a thoroughfare designed to by pass nearby small towns. It was constructed for members of the human race in a hurry to reach their destination. But for those who want to "see" this part of Alberta, travel down Highway #2A. Though it is narrow and mostly shoulder-less (some sections are being widened), this is where the sights are.

Stop in at Kilborn Antiques in Millet, to see grandfather clocks, rolltop desks, table and chair sets, dishes, and lamps.

You can't visit Wetaskiwin without stopping in at the Reynold's Alberta Museum, with its collection of antique cars, trucks, tractors, steam engines, fire engines, war artifacts, and airplanes.

Ponoka is well-known for its annual stampede, held on the July long weekend. During the summer, the Ponoka Stampede Museum is open in the tourist information booth.

Red Deer is famous for its parks structure. You can hike or bicycle all across the city on paths connecting the smaller parks of the Waskasoo Park system.

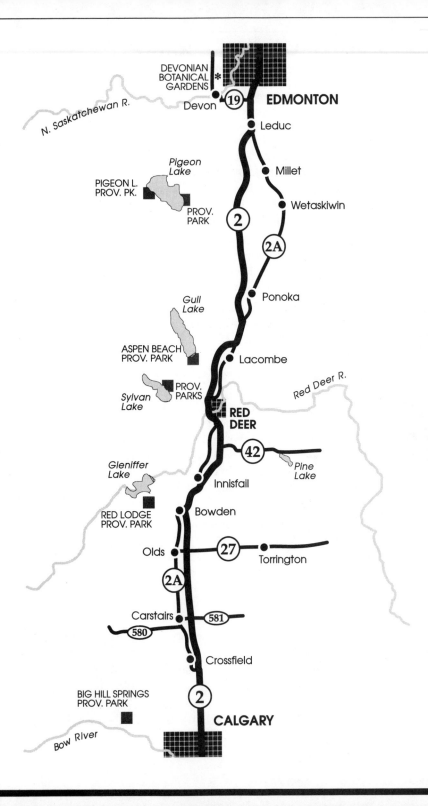

Devon to Lacombe

Devon is not located on #2A but is a good beginning for the drive. Oil was struck about one kilometre (0.6 miles) south of here in 1947, and this well was the start of the Leduc-Woodbend oil field. The new town that quickly sprang up was called Devon, after the Devonian rock formation base in which the oil was discovered. The Leduc Oil Field is now famous throughout the world.

On the site, one kilometre (0.6 miles) south of the town, is the Leduc #1 oil derrick, on the east side of Highway #60. The derrick is actually an antique similar to the original used to drill that Discovery well.

Native Peoples' Garden, Devonian Botanic Gardens

Devon holds a raft race down the North Saskatchewan River in the summer. In the winter, the Nordic Ski Club operates a 55 metre (180 foot) and a 25 metre (80 foot) ski jump, for experts as well as beginners.

Drive five kilometres (three miles) north of Devon, through the North Saskatchewan River valley with its red banks and green trees, to the University of Alberta Devonian Botanic Gardens. Park in the large, flower-decorated lot and visit the gift shop for information before striking out on your tramp through the woods.

The gardens were developed by the University in 1959 and have several trails leading to many contrasting plant and animal communities. Some of the sections you will see are a five acre Japanese garden, a herb garden, a Native people's garden, desert plants, a peony collection, and woody ornamentals.

The walk is enjoyable, but remember that the garden is in a natural setting and has many of the hazards of a regular forest. Watch for wet ground, tree roots, and mosquitoes.

Japanese Garden, Devonian Botanic Gardens

LEDUC

Drive south of Devon on Highway #60 to Highway #39. Turn east and head for Leduc. Many of the towns of Alberta received their names from Catholic priests who served the communities. Leduc is one such town. When the postmaster opened his office, he wanted a name for it but had a hard time picking one. Finally, one day he decided to name it after the first person who walked in the door. Father Leduc, who had walked many miles in the cold, stopped in at the office to warm up and the town's name was set.

Leduc #1 Well

In an effort to encourage the food preparation industry in the province, a food processing centre, sponsored by the Government of Alberta, was established in Leduc. Facilities, technical expertise, equipment, and financial help are available to food processors. At the centre, companies are able to fully analyze their proposed food preparation methods, before making any large investment.

MILLET

Stop in at Kilborn Antiques in Millet, to see grandfather clocks, rolltop desks, table and chair sets, dishes, and lamps. The owners travel all over Canada in search of antiques for their business. They have a personal glassware collection consisting of cutglass dating back to the early 1900s, dishes, and lamps from the 1880s. Occasionally, they display this collection at the Millet museum.

WETASKIWIN

The Legend of Wetaskiwin-Spatinow

One day, a war party of Blackfoot and a war party of Cree were unknowingly riding towards each other. That night they camped on opposite sides of a hill. A young chief from one band decided to scout the hill. At the top he met a chief from the other band and they immediately began wrestling. They struggled for many hours before pausing to rest. • The Blackfoot lit his pipe, but when the Cree went to light his, he found that it had been broken in the scuffle. The Blackfoot offered his; the Cree accepted and began puffing. They suddenly realized they had just smoked the pipe of peace. Each quickly returned to his camp and related the tale to the other members of the band. • Everyone felt it was a sign that peace should be made. Chiefs from both tribes assembled and passed the peace pipe from mouth to mouth. That hill became known as Wetaskiwin-Spatinow — "the hill where peace was made."

During the North West (Riel) Rebellion in 1885, the Alberta Field Force build Fort Ethier, a blockhouse on land owned by the Lucas family, five miles north of present-day Wetaskiwin. When the threat of war subsided, the fort was used as a stop-over house on the Edmonton-Calgary trail.

The blockhouse still stands today. It is small but has two storeys — the ground floor about 1.2 metres (four feet) high and a top level, not much higher. The second storey has 12 loopholes through which soldiers could fire at the rebels. These defences proved unnecessary, as not one shot was discharged in the battle at the fort. You may obtain directions to the farm at the information booth in Wetaskiwin, but the blockhouse is on private land, so you should phone ahead if you want to visit.

Fort Ethier

You can't visit Wetaskiwin without stopping in at the Reynold's Alberta Museum, with its collection of antique cars, trucks, tractors, steam engines, fire engines, war artifacts, and airplanes. It was first opened to the public in 1955 under the name Reynold's Museum. Over the years, it has expanded and was finally moved to a new site, three minutes west of the city on Highway 13.

The oldest aircraft at the museum is a 1918 Curtiss JN4 Canuck. It was christened the "City of Edmonton" and was piloted by Wop May and George Gorman until 1924. Its last flight was in the 1930s.

Wetaskiwin isn't noted just for its vintage vehicles. The town has the highest per capita automotive sales in Canada and is known as the car capital of the country. Drive the "Automile" and maybe you can make a deal on a vehicle while you are in town.

Ponoka

Ponoka is well-known for its annual stampede, held on the July long weekend. During the summer, the Ponoka Stampede Museum is open in the tourist information booth. Saddles, a young Native woman in full dress, trophies, a chuck wagon, and many old photographs of the rodeo are on exhibit. Inhale deeply and savour the aroma of old leather blended with a trace of tanned hide.

Ponoka is also the home of the Fort Ostell Museum. Fort Ostell was one of the posts established by the Alberta Field Force during the North West (Riel) Rebellion. There are picnic tables set on a large lawn and a fishing pond at the museum.

The Alberta Hospital at Ponoka has been in operation since
1911. It is a regional psychiatric treatment complex for central
and southern Alberta. Throughout its history, it has worked to
change the attitudes of society toward the mentally ill and to
provide a high standard of patient care. It also is renowned for
its training of psychiatric nurses.

LACOMBE

Lacombe was named after Father Albert Lacombe, a Roman
Catholic missionary who spent
his life working among the Native people. As part of its
Mainstreet Project, the town has
restored many of its historic
buildings, some of which were

Michener House, Lacombe

constructed in the early 1900s. One of the more prominent structures is the Michener House where Daniel Roland Michener, Governor-General of Canada from 1967 to 1974, was born in 1900.

Roland Michener

Roland Michener graduated from the University of Alberta with the highest standing in the province, received a Rhodes Scholarship, and attended Hertford College in England, where he earned his law degree. He became involved in politics in the late 1930s and enjoyed a long life in the political field. He was elected to the House of Commons in 1953, was appointed High Commissioner to India in 1964 and Canadian Ambassador to Nepal in 1965, and was named Governor General in 1967. Always active in sports, he was known as "Canada's jogging Governor General." • The Alberta government named a mountain after him in 1979 (*Chapter 10*, Nordegg to Banff National Park section) and in 1982, at the age of 82, he climbed his mountain.

Red Deer and District

Red Deer is famous for its parks structure. You can hike or bicycle all across the city on paths connecting the smaller parks of the Waskasoo Park system. Each park has its own unique attractions.

At the Bower Ponds in Great Chief Park you can rent canoes, paddle boats, and fishing tackle. On the bank overlooking the ponds is Cronquist House. The three storey, 325 square metre (3500 square foot) Victorian structure was built in 1912.

Cronquist House, Red Deer

When Cronquist House was threatened with demolition in 1976, the Red Deer International Folk Festival Society decided to save it by relocating it. They stripped the bricks from the outside and removed the inside plaster. Then, while the Red Deer River was still frozen, they skidded it down the steep bank, across the ice, and up the other side to the Bower Ponds. Take a tour through the completely restored house, which is now a multicultural centre with exhibits, workshops, classes, a library, and a meeting room.

The Red Deer International Folk Festival is held on the July long weekend in the Great Chief Park. Many ethno-cultural groups from central Alberta gather for the celebration. Red Deer held its first folk festival in 1969.

Some of the other parks in the system are the Maskepetoon Athletic Park, the Rotary Park, the Great West Adventure Park, Heritage Ranch, and Fort Normandeau. The present Fort Normandeau is a replica, although some of the logs from the original were used in its construction. The fort is on the banks of the Red Deer River, west of Highway #2. It is linked to the other parks, first by river to Heritage Ranch, and then by trail to Great Chief Park.

Heritage Ranch offers trail, pony, and winter sleigh rides, and a viewing tower from which you can see the city centre and the Red Deer River.

Fort Normandeau

The walking tour of Red Deer covers 4.5 kilometres (2.8 miles) and takes you past more than 25 historical sites and buildings. In an effort to preserve the area's heritage while keeping up with modern times, the downtown Bank of Montreal set aside two corbels and a sandstone block from the original bank building, constructed in 1913. The corbels now hang on each side of the new entrance and the sandstone block lies in a flower bed in front of the doors.

One of Alberta's great architectural achievements is St. Mary's Church in Red Deer. It was designed by architect Douglas Cardinal and completed in 1968. The pattern was inspired by a spider's web. The exterior is flowing and semi-circular; the interior focuses on the alter with the aisles branching in different directions.

If downhill skiing is what you like, visit the Canyon Ski Area east of Red Deer on #595. This is the largest non-mountain ski resort in Alberta. It has two chairlifts, two T-bars, and a handle tow to get you

St. Mary's Church

up to the top. You then have a choice of 11 runs down the canyon of the Red Deer River.

Pine Lake, near Red Deer, is very popular with the residents of the area. To reach the lake, head south on Highway #2 to #42 and turn east. Follow the highway to Ghost Pine Trail and turn south. Resorts, a hotel, service stations, a dude ranch and campground, restaurant, store, day use only government campground, other campgrounds, and a trailer park are just some of the facilities at the lake. The Ghost Pine Lake Resort has the added feature of an indoor swimming pool. There is also a Salvation Army camp and a Prairie Bible Institute camp on the shores of the lake.

Ghost Pine Lake

According to legend, a party of Blackfoot massacred a camp of Cree on the shore of this lake in the early 1800s. One Cree warrior, who had been hunting, returned and found his family and friends dead. He painted his face black in mourning and began to stalk the Blackfoot. By entering their camp at night or attacking a lone brave, he was able to kill and scalp many enemies. The Blackfoot, thinking it was a ghost killing the braves, quickly fled the shores of what was thereafter known as Ghost Pine Lake or Devil's Pine Lake.

Innisfail to Crossfield

INNISFAIL

Innisfail was a popular layover on the Calgary to Edmonton trail in the 1880s. The only preserved stopping house from that era is in the historic village at Innisfail. The house was built in 1886 and was visited by stage coaches running the trail.

Innisfail also has the Hereford Breeding Test Centre. Based on 29 hectares (72 acres), it has the capacity to board up to 72 bulls at one time. The main objective of the centre is to improve the Hereford breed.

Innisfail Historical Village

Northwest of Innisfail is the high ground of Antler Ridge. It is from this ridge that Anthony Henday became the first European to see the Rocky Mountains.

BOWDEN

Between Innisfail and Bowden, Highways #2A and #2 merge into Highway #2. Just before the town of Bowden, on the east side of the highway is the only RCMP dog training facility in Canada. Dogs are trained for every major law enforcement agency in the country and are taught obedience, agility, and criminal apprehension. Take a tour of the facility and view the instruction procedure.

If you like your fruit fresh and enjoy picking it, head west of Bowden on #587 to Pearson's U-pick Berry Farm. You can select your own strawberries in July, saskatoons from the end of July to the middle of August, and raspberries in August. There is also a limited supply of chokecherries, pincherries, currants, and hi-bush cranberries.

OLDS

Olds College has played an important role in Alberta's agricultural development since its opening in 1913. Tours of the campus and farm are available, and you will see rose gardens, landscaped lawns, and botanical green spaces. If you feel the need for exercise after hours of driving, the college's fitness centre is open to the public year round.

For hunters, Mountainview Taxidermy in Olds prepares life-size mounts of animals, birds in flight, fish, game heads, and the taxidermists will make rugs from skins and mount horns.

The A.H. Johnson ranch operates the Tack Corral in Olds, where you can buy new and used tack and saddles. For the first time horse owner, the ranch also holds clinics on green colt training, beginner jumping, and beginner riding, and has trail riding camps.

The Mountain View Handicapped Riding Association sponsors riding lessons for mentally and physically disabled people. The lessons are held from May to August on Tuesday and Thursday evenings at the Olds Cow Palace.

DIDSBURY

South of Olds, at Didsbury, are three excellent Bed and Break-fasts. For those who prefer to stay in town there is the Pengary House at 1610 15 Avenue. This B&B is open year round and has wheelchair access to the Tea Room.

For a country setting try the Ausenhus B&B, which is 4 kilo-metres (2.5 miles) east of town on secondary road #582. They offer late afternoon tea besides breakfast. If you prefer an active stay, the West Way Hide-A-Way B&B will give you a chance to spend a day on a working farm. Phone 335-4929 for direction to the farm.

CARSTAIRS

Most towns have fairs and exhibitions—Carstairs has the Great Pumpkin Festival, in the last weekend of September. Growers for miles around spend their summers carefully cultivating

Atlantic Giants, hoping to receive first prize. The winning pumpkin the first year weighed 148 kilograms (326 pounds) and that record hasn't been broken.

Besides the pumpkin challenge, there is the King and Queen contest. Entrants have to draw the best pumpkin, carve a pumpkin, and outdo the others at pie eating. Another competition requires contestants to design an outfit for a pumpkin. The festivities end with a pioneer supper and dance.

Would you like to try your hand at growing and entering one of these great orange vegetables? There are three classes: Carstairs and area, the rest of the province, and outside the province. A pumpkin plumping tip: saturating the roots with milk is supposed to guarantee enormous growth.

Another attraction in Carstairs is its famous fudge. Stop in at the store on Main Street for a sample or purchase some from the booth at the Calgary Stampede.

A monument to Henry Wise Wood is on Hammond Street and 11th Avenue. Wood was a promoter of a strong farm organization and was president of the United Farmers' Association for 15 years.

Sheep

One of the oldest known domesticated animal is the sheep. Shepherds were guarding flocks against predators long before recorded history. Originally tamed for their hides and milk, and to carry burdens, sheep were carefully bred to replace their coarse hair with soft wool. This soft wool has been used for centuries in the making of material for clothing. • Alberta's sheep industry, with an annual production of over 567,000 kilograms (1 1/4 million pounds) of wool, is the most extensive in Canada.

Near Carstairs are two craft shops which make products from sheep wool. One, Pasu Farms, is southwest of Carstairs on #580; the other, Custom Woolen Mills is east on #581.

At Pasu Farms, the owners display weavings from Africa and sell tapestries, carvings, stuffed sheep toys, moccasins with sheep skin linings, hand knitted sweaters, mens' vests, coats, and many more items created from the sheep's wool. You could spend hours looking at the exhibits and then go on a tour of the working part of the farm. If you like being creative, craft classes are offered in the fall and winter.

Some of the machinery used by Custom Woolen Mills in the manufacture of products for knitting, quilting, and spinning could be considered old. The spinning mule was made in 1910 and the five carding machines date from 1867 to 1910. The comforter sewing machine was constructed in the mid 1900s.

The comforters made at Custom Mills are filled with 100% pure, virgin, Canadian wool. Because it is grown in a cold climate, it is fluffier than foreign wool. For those who live in the snow belt, soft, warm wool covers are great to snuggle under on frosty winter nights.

CROSSFIELD

When you enter the town of Crossfield, you are on the highest point of land between Calgary and Edmonton. A two storey high mural of a cowboy riding a bucking bronco is painted on the wall of the Crossfield AG Foods. Their rodeo, held during the first week in July, is called Pete Knight Days in honour of a world famous Alberta cowboy of the 1930s.

Chapter 9

Drayton Valley to Canmore

This section is one of the best hunting and fishing regions in Alberta. You will weave through parkland and foothills on your journey and see mainly bush and farms.

Three campgrounds at Brazeau Dam have, altogether, over 300 stalls. There are rainbow trout, brown trout, pickerel, and Rocky Mountain whitefish in the waters of the area. Elk, moose, and deer abound and wild strawberries, raspberries, cranberries, and blueberries are waiting for pickers.

Besides the birds common to this area, some rare ones such as arctic loons, mew gulls, and parasitic jaegers, can also be seen at Pigeon Lake. Whitefish, pike, jack, and pickerel are plentiful in the lake.

At the Dickson Dam across the Red Deer River, there is an information display, a picnic area, and a viewing area at the site. There is good fishing at Gleniffer Lake in both summer and winter, and loons, geese, swans, and ducks visit the lake. Watch, too, for moose and deer.

The Raven River and Stauffer Creek (North Raven) are two of the best brown trout streams in Alberta. In the James and Clearwater Rivers, you can try for whitefish, brown and bull trout. You might also catch a brook trout in the Clearwater. Struble lake has trout, while Burnstick Lake has perch and pike.

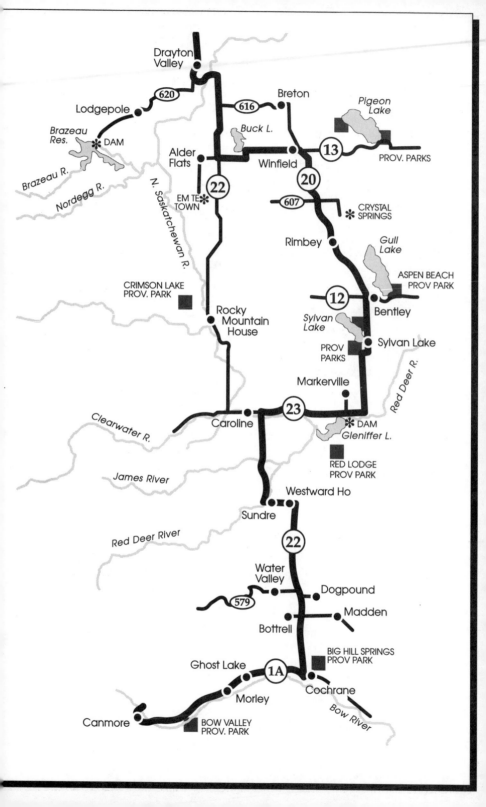

Drayton Valley to Rimbey

DRAYTON VALLEY

Drayton Valley is 42 kilometres (25 miles) south of Highway #16, and owes its existence to oil. The Pembina oil field near this town cost over $900 million to develop—more money than was spent on the St. Lawrence Seaway. Because of this oil field, Drayton Valley, with 13 operating pumpjacks within the town limits, has one of the highest incomes per capita in Canada.

North Saskatchewan River at Drayton Valley

The town is the principal trading centre for the companies looking after 8,000 wells, 1,500 oil production facilities, thousands of kilometres of buried pipe, 53 sweet gas plants, and 24 sour gas plants.

Besides oil, Drayton Valley has a large forestry industry. The Pelican Spruce Mills, which produces "sturdi-wood" from poplar trees, is situated in the southwest corner of town. Pelican has an output of 23.1 million square metres (250 million square feet) of product a year—enough wood for about 60,000 homes. Beside the Pelican factory is a dimensional lumber mill, which yields enough board feet of lumber in a year to construct 10,000 homes.

BRAZEAU DAM

Because the flow of water varies with the seasons (low in winter) and Edmonton and other communities needed an assured energy source throughout the year, the Brazeau Dam was erected on the Brazeau River. The river is a tributary of the North Saskatchewan River and is southwest of Drayton Valley. The project was completed in 1961, with an extension added in 1969.

Go south on Highway #22 and turn onto #620. Travel through Lodgepole and continue on the gravel road to the dam. Three campgrounds at the site have, altogether, over 300 stalls. There are rainbow trout, brown trout, pickerel, and Rocky Mountain whitefish in the waters of the area. Elk, moose, and deer abound and wild strawberries, raspberries, cranberries, and blueberries are waiting for pickers. You can hike the numerous trails in the summer or cross-country ski and snowmobile in the winter.

To arrive back at Highway #22, you should return through Lodgepole. The roads that look as if they will take you across country are either oil or logging arteries, so be careful; if you take one you may get lost.

BRETON

Back on Highway #22, cross the North Saskatchewan River and travel east until the highway turns south. Twelve kilometres (7.5 miles) south is Highway #616, leading to Breton. The town was established in the early 1900s, and many of its first settlers were black immigrants from Oklahoma. The Keystone Cemetery, north of the town, was begun by these settlers and some of their history can be found in the Breton Historical Museum.

EM TE TOWN

To see a Wild West town, continue south on Highway #22. Three kilometres (1.8 miles) south of the junction with Highway #13, turn west and drive 10 kilometres (6 miles) to Em Te Town. The parking lot is a short distance from the town. Walk across a small bridge, then follow a path through a field.

The town has two streets with buildings down both sides. A wooden sidewalk connects the log structures, and hitching rails are just waiting for cowboys to tie up their horses.

Em Te began with one man, who lived in a tent, putting up a log cabin. From there, he continued to construct buildings

Em Te Town

until he had a small town. The second owner added a few more structures to round out the town and now there is a saloon, a music store, a hotel, the home of Walksfar Woman, and a variety of other period structures. Stroll into the buildings and inhale the fresh scent of the wood. With the help of authentic furnishings, it is easy to imagine yourself in the Wild West of the 1800s.

BUCK LAKE AND PIGEON LAKE

If you want to laze away a summer afternoon, rent a houseboat on Buck Lake, lay back in the sunshine, and enjoy the gentle rocking of the waves. Or if you prefer fishing, the lake has whitefish, pike, and perch.

Pigeon Lake Provincial Park

For those who like more activity, head east of Buck Lake to Pigeon Lake. There are eight summer villages and two provincial campgrounds on this body of water. There are two 18-hole golf courses, at Mulhurst and Ma-Me-O Beach. Mulhurst also has a driving range, miniature golf, and equipment rentals.

Besides the birds common to the area, some rare ones such as arctic loons, mew gulls, and parasitic jaegers, can also be seen at Pigeon Lake. Whitefish, pike, jack, and pickerel are plentiful in the lake.

Cheese

From Pigeon Lake, go west on Highway #13 to Highway #20, turn south, and drive about 23 kilometres (14 miles) to Highway #607. On the fence post is a sign with one word: Cheese. Turn east and drive about seven kilometres (four miles) to another sign pointing south. A quarter of a kilometre down the road is Crystal Springs Cheese Farm. • Crystal Springs is privately owned and the owners produce many unusual types of cheese for customers with different tastes. While you wait, look through the window into the back room; that white liquid in the large vat is whey, the watery portion of milk that separates from the solids when cheese is made. Pictures on the wall portray the cheese-making process. • There are many flavors to chose from: swiss, cow feta, gouda, spiced, and mild, medium, and old goat. You may buy as many different samples of cheese as you wish, in what ever size you think you can eat. The spiced variety is especially delicious.

RIMBEY

Back on Highway #20, head south to Rimbey. For the early settlers, the only method of hauling grain, animals, and supplies to and from the market at Lacombe was by team and wagon. In 1910, fed up by the long distance and slow transportation, they began formulating plans for a private railroad to be called the Farmer's and Merchant's Line.

Pas Ka Poo, Rimbey

The project was put on hold during the war but quickly resumed at the war's end. By the fall of 1919, Lacombe and Rimbey were linked by rail. The line was then extended north to Hoadley and Winfield in 1923. The railroad, termed the Peanut Special, Muskeg Special, and the Lacombe and Blindman Valley Electric Railway Company by the district's inhabitants, operated until the 1960s.

The Blindman River, south of Rimbey, is good for canoeing or pike fishing.

Bentley to Madden

BENTLEY AND GULL LAKE

The Medicine Hills, west of Bentley, were once a focal point for Native religious practices. Today, they are the location of the Medicine Lodge Ski Hill. If you like to walk, take the four kilometre (2.5 mile) path from Bentley to Gull Lake.

Gull Lake was formed when glaciers melted thousands of years ago. It is smaller than it once was, but there are still 51 kilometres (30 miles) of lake shore, much of it sandy beaches.

Aspen Beach, on Gull Lake, was originally called Weitesville, after a German pioneer, but was renamed during the First World War. Aspen Beach Provincial Park, created in 1932, was Alberta's first provincial park.

From Bentley, continue south on Highway #20 to Sylvan Lake (see *Chapter 10*, Sylvan Lake to Leslieville section). Take Highway #781 south to Highway #54. Turn west and watch for the signs to the historic site of Markerville.

Sylvan Lake

MARKERVILLE

Markerville is famous for its creamery, established in 1899. In 1902, because of increased demand, the present building was constructed on the banks of the Medicine River. The creamery produced award-winning butter until it closed in 1972. It is now an historic site, with a gift and coffee shop, and is the only restored creamery in Alberta.

Take a guided tour of the creamery, or wander through it on your own. Make sure you lean into the large wooden, butter churn and inhale the rich aroma of cream still lingering in the wood.

In the hamlet, a huge cream can overlooks the Medicine River. The plaque reads:

1888-1988
Dedicated to the pioneers of Markerville and District
who prepared the way.
"They did so much with so little."
The best that was in me forever shall live.
The sun over darkness prevails.

Stephan G. Stephansson.

Lilly Seigfried

Stephan Stephansson's granddaughter, Lilly Seigfried, lives in Markerville. She is shy but loves to talk about the old Stephansson house and her memories of visits to her grandparents as a young girl. She has a photograph of the house when it was still a natural wood colour and is not impressed with the current pink and green paint job.

North of Markerville is another historic site — the restored home of Stephan G. Stephansson. The Stephannson house has been restored to its 1927 appearance. A young girl in period clothes will greet you at the door and take you on a tour of the house.

Stephansson House, north of Markerville

In one room, a spinning wheel awaits a spinner and a basket of wool requires carding. The interpreter will demonstrate how the early settlers carded their wool by using two large toothed brushes to straighten and separate the fibres. Try your hand at the art; it isn't as easy as it looks.

Each day, a batch of cookies is baked in an old wood stove in the kitchen. If you are lucky enough to arrive when the cookies are being removed from the oven, you will get to sample some fresh, homemade, Icelandic fare. The recipe is printed on cards for those wishing to make their own.

Stephan G. Stephansson

Stephansson was born in Northern Iceland in 1853. Because of poverty, he didn't attend school and his parents taught him to read and write. The brutal climate finally drove them to immigrate to the United States in 1873. • After a dispute with their church in 1889, Stephansson, his wife and children, and a few other families moved to land southwest of Red Deer. He homesteaded and wrote poetry, most of which was in Icelandic. • In 1909, Iceland saluted him as its greatest poet since the 13th century. When his poems were translated into English, Canada also recognized him as one of the country's primary poets.

Drive back to Highway #54 and turn south to the Dickson Dam across the Red Deer River. There is an information display, a picnic area, and a viewing area at the site. There is good fishing at Gleniffer Lake in both summer and winter, and loons, geese, swans, and ducks visit the lake. Watch, too, for moose and deer.

Continue on Highway #54 to Caroline, hometown of World Figure Skating Chapmion, Kurt Browning. Drop into the Kurt Browning Arena on 51st St. and see his memorabilia in "Kurt's Korner." For handcrafted gifts, head 7 kilometres (4.3 miles) south on Highway #22, then east 2.6 kilometres (1.6 miles) to The Cabin.

The Caroline Elks Club hosts an annual big game supper each fall. On the menu are elk, moose, antelope, bear, partridge, turkey, goose, and any other wild meat the members of the club shot during hunting season. Everyone is welcome to come and taste the distinct flavours of the meats.

Kurt Browning

Kurt Browning, the Canadian Men's Figure Skating Champion and the World Figure Skating Champion for 1989-90-91, was born and raised on a ranch near Caroline. Kurt was also voted Canada's Male Athlete of 1990—the first figure skater to be awarded the title.

Eleven kilometres (7 miles) southeast of Caroline on Highway #22 is the Raven Brook Trout Station. Thousands of trout are hatched here, then sent to the fish hatchery in Calgary. From there, the fish are used to stock lakes and streams throughout the province. There is a campsite, but no overnight camping.

This area is ideal for avid fishermen. The Raven River and Stauffer Creek (North Raven) are two of the best brown trout streams in Alberta. In the James and Clearwater Rivers, you can try for whitefish, brown and bull trout. You might also catch a brook trout in the Clearwater. Struble Lake has trout, while Burnstick Lake has perch and pike.

Brown trout

SUNDRE, WESTWARD HO AND WATER VALLEY

The Red Deer River, near Sundre, has some of the top whitewater rafting and canoeing in Canada. Many rafting companies in Sundre offer trips down the river. For less brave visitors, there is an 18-hole golf course. History buffs will enjoy the Pioneer Museum and its collection of pioneer artifacts and farm machinery.

Westward Ho is an 800 site campground named after Charles Kingsley's famous novel. About 35 kilometres (22 miles) south of

Westward Ho is Highway #579 and Water Valley is just a few kilometres west. Some locals say it should actually be known as Whiskey Valley or Moonshine Valley because this was the location of the still which operated during prohibition in the late 1920s and supplied Calgary with most of its bootleg liquor.

DOGPOUND AND MADDEN

If you are in the area in July and want to take in the oldest stampede in Alberta, watch for the sign for Dogpound as you continue south. It is a small community that, for many years, was a Cree camp and hunting ground. Now it is famous for the Dogpound Rodeo.

East of Bottrell, on Highway #574, is the town of Madden and the Madden Buffalo Jump. Go south 3.2 kilometres (two miles), east five kilometres (3.1 miles), then north one kilometre (0.6 miles) to get to the site. Archaeologists believe that the Shoshoni camped and hunted here in the 1600s and that they drew pictographs on the rocks to tell their stories.

Cochrane to Canmore

COCHRANE

Cochrane was named after Senator Matthew Cochrane, who started the first large-scale cattle ranch in Alberta. In 1881, he had a herd of 7,000 cattle brought up from Montana. During the long, hard drive, many of them died and most of the remaining ones perished during the winter. Five thousand more head were driven up under the same conditions the next year and by the third year there were only about 4,000 head left of the original 12,000. The ranch became known as the Hard Luck Ranch. In 1883, it was sold to another Cochrane syndicate, and the remaining herd was driven south to a new lease in the Fort Macleod/Belly River district.

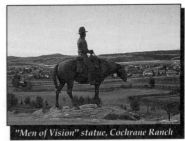

"Men of Vision" statue, Cochrane Ranch

Today, the Cochrane Ranch is a provincial park and nature preserve with a visitors' centre, corral, viewing area, and self-guiding trails. On a bluff overlooking the corral is the 3.7 metre (12 foot) high "Men of Vision" sculpture. The statue, a man astride a horse, is a memorial to the men who lived and worked Alberta ranches so many years ago.

Visit the Western Heritage Centre, where you can trace the history of the cattle industry in the West — from cattle drives to feedlots, and rodeos to auctions. The total ranch area is 60 hectares (150 acres), so be prepared to stay a while.

The Open Range

The southern Alberta plains were once covered by a highly nutritive, self-curing mixture of gamma, blue-joint, and other grasses, called prairie wool. When the settlers realized the value of the grasses for livestock during the 1870s, the era of cowboys, trail drives, and rustlers began. • Reverend John McDougall and his brother, David, arrived at Morley with 50 head of horses and cattle in 1873. This was believed to be the first livestock in Alberta. They brought another 100 head of steers and breeding stock from Fort Benton the following year. • Two hundred more head of Montana stock arrived in the Fort Macleod area in 1878. Soon, large trail drives were organized and at their completion, many of the drovers stayed in Alberta to establish their own ranches. Some Mounties also took up ranching when their terms with the NWMP expired. So did former buffalo hunters, traders, and new immigrants. • As the buffalo were depleted, starving Natives took to shooting cattle for food. To curtail the slaughter, the government rented out land for one cent an acre, removed the duty on cattle brought to the plains, and bought the finished animal as food for the natives. With this policy in place, the ranching industry developed at a great speed. By 1890, more than 115,000 cattle were roaming the country south of the Little Red Deer River. • But raising cattle was not easy. There were range fires, rustlers, wolves, and hard winters to worry about. The winters of 1886-87 and 1906-07 were two of the worst. Alberta lost half of its cattle to the blizzards, cold, and heavy snow of 1906-07 and many ranchers never recovered from their losses. • In the early 1900s, Alberta was the sight of the last land rush of North America. The Native people had been on reserves since 1880 and posed little threat. The North West Mounted Police were present and the railroad had been completed in 1885. The federal and provincial governments strongly encouraged migration west. • The first surge of settlers headed to the open prairie east and south of Calgary. The next took land further north in the rolling parkland. By 1910, the homesteading boom was under way and many acres of prairie wool disappeared under the plow. In order to retain their spreads, ranchers had to purchase the land and erect barbed wire fences to secure their cattle. • After less than 40 years duration, the magnificence and romance of the open range was no more.

If you are a hang gliding enthusiast, or just like to watch, Big Hill is one of the finest locations in western Canada for the sport. You can take paragliding lessons at the hill or rent equipment from Paragliding Canada.

Cochrane itself is an excellent town for someone who appreciates the arts. There is a pottery studio, an antique shop, and many galleries displaying dolls, fine arts, crafts, paintings, and bronze sculptures. History buffs will want to take the walking tour of Cochrane.

The houses, churches, hotels, and lodges date back to the late 1800s and early 1900s. One such structure is MacKay's Ice Cream Store. The building was constructed between 1900 and 1910 and was bought in 1948 by Jimmy MacKay. He began producing and selling ice cream soon after he moved in, and the original recipe has not been altered over the past decades. Try some — it was rated second best in Canada on a taste test done by CTV's "Live It Up" current affairs program.

If you have a hankering for an Old West atmosphere when you dine, visit the Texas Gate Restaurant. You can order Texas fried chicken or belly-up to the smorgasbord. Dance later to country and western music.

There are many guest ranches along Highway #1A where you can choose a short horseback ride, a camping trip on horseback, or riding lessons. The monument on the side of the road is dedicated to a Canadian and an American fighter pilot who died in the Second World War.

Just a few kilometres past the monument is the Ghost Dam on the Bow River. The Ghost Reservoir is stocked with rainbow trout and the Bow River, which runs beside the highway to Canmore, has Rocky Mountain whitefish and rainbow and brown trout.

After Ghost Lake, watch for the tall, lone church enclosed by a rail fence on the south side of the road. This is the McDougall Memorial United Church. Built in 1875, it was named after Reverend George McDougall and his son Reverend John McDougall. This father and son missionary team devoted a total of 77 years to the well-being of the Natives of western Canada.

McDougall Memorial Church, 1875

George McDougall, who died in a blizzard, rests in a grave beside the church. John retired to Calgary in 1906 and wrote several books before his death in 1917.

The sign over the gate into the yard reads "Remove Not The Ancient Landmark Which Thy Fathers Have Set."

If it is late afternoon or early evening and you are thinking about quitting for the day, stop in at the Stoney Indian Park Campground. For a unique experience, rent a tipi, which will sleep 6 to 8 people. Wander through the site to some of the lookout points where you can view the Bow River, the mountains, and maybe a buffalo in the paddock below. A monument to one Stoney who died during the Second World War stands on the grounds.

Canmore was established as a coal mining town in 1883 and some historic buildings from that era are still in use. Although Canmore began as a coal town, it is now a major service centre for Kananaskis Country.

The town was the sight of the 1988 Olympic cross-country skiing, biathlon, and nordic-combined competitions. If you like windsurfing, try nearby Lac Des Arcs. The winds blowing across the lake have given it high standing with those who enjoy the sport.

Chapter 10
Sylvan Lake to Nordegg

Travel this route and you will meander through rolling parkland and deep forests; past lakes and over streams filled with perch, rainbow trout, mountain whitefish, and walleye; through big game country; and near falls and canyons. This scenic highway was named after an equally impressive man, David Thompson.

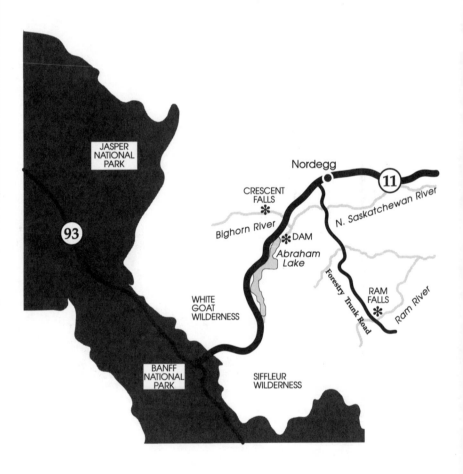

If you are an entomologist, you will be interested in watching for the rare southern black witch moth, which has been seen in the vicinity of Sylvan and Cygnet Lakes.

Evarts, south of Highway #11 on Spruceview Road, was the original stopover for freight wagons travelling between Red Deer and Rocky Mountain House in the early 1900's. The only evidence that Evarts ever existed is the Historical Cairn.

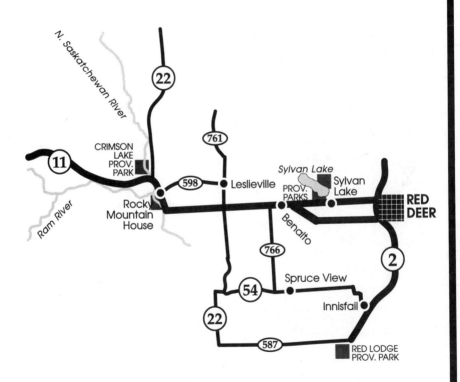

Sylvan Lake to Leslieville

David Thompson, who spent 28 years working as a fur trader and exploring and mapping western Canada, has been called the greatest land geographer who ever lived. He was a genius at mathematics and so accurate with his calculations of latitude and longitude that he could chart the courses of rivers, pinpoint the locations of lakes, and accurately report the positions of mountain ranges.

He was employed by the Hudson's Bay Company for 10 years, then spent 18 years with the North West Company. In those 28 years of exploring, surveying, mapping, and fur trading in western Canada, he travelled 50,000 miles on foot, and by canoe, dog sled, and pack horse.

In 1802, Thompson left Rocky Mountain House on the first of many trips through the mountains. He discovered a route to the headwaters of the Columbia River in British Columbia in 1807. In the fall of 1810, he cut a road overland from the North Saskatchewan River, below Rocky Mountain House, to the Athabasca River. He ascended the river, discovered the Athabasca Pass, and reached the site of modern-day Jasper.

On the trip over the pass, he lost a sack containing 114 musket balls. A search proved fruitless and Thompson decided they must have been carried off by a wolverine. In August 1921, 114 severely corroded musket balls were found slightly north of the summit of the pass by a member of the Interprovincial Boundary Commission.

Thompson spent the years 1813-14 composing a map of the North West Territory. This accurate chart laid the foundation for all future survey work in the area. He died on Feb. 10, 1857, penniless and in relative obscurity.

Liquor

Thompson did not drink liquor and, unlike most of his fellow traders, did not believe in using it for barter. On one trip into the Kootenays, he was given two kegs of rum to distribute to the Natives. He refused the kegs, but was ordered to carry them. He obediently tied them onto a packhorse and embarked on his journey. • The horse, his most excitable animal, resented the extra weight and did its best to knock the kegs off by banging them against trees and rocks. It wasn't long before the kegs were broken and the rum was dampening the dust of the trail. That was the only time Thompson was charged with the task of transporting liquor.

Sylvan Lake itself has attracted visitors since 1901 and the resort town has been in existence since 1913. The beaches are crowded all summer and there are many recreational activities and attractions for both the young and those who think young.

The Sandy Cove Fun Centre has a crazy maze, mini golf, trampolines, and much more to keep children occupied. For thrill seekers, the Wild Rapids Water Slide, Canada's largest free-standing water slide, is open every day. Take in one of the greyhound races held throughout the summer or visit the only operating lighthouse between Winnipeg and the west coast. The beacon was erected on the shore of Sylvan Lake to commemorate the town's 75th anniversary.

Sylvan Lake Marina

If you are an entomologist, you will be interested in watching for the rare southern black witch moth, which has been seen in the vicinity of Sylvan and Cygnet Lakes.

BENALTO

Continue west on Highway #11 to Benalto. Drive south through this hamlet to the Earth Works studio of Betty Neilson. She is a multi-talented woman who is a potter, a weaver, and a painter.

Mrs. Neilson has three looms on the second floor of her studio —one large, one small, and one for tapestry—and each always has a work in progress on it. She produces capes, sweaters, shirts, and cushion covers. Without any prompting, she will sit down at one of the looms and demonstrate the art of weaving. Another room on the same floor contains her sewing machine, countless balls of yarn, and a spinning wheel.

Her works are displayed on the ground floor, and her potter's wheel is in the basement. She will choose a piece of clay and "throw" a beautiful bowl while you watch. When she has completed the task, she will nonchalantly crumple it up and return the clay to its bag while you gasp in dismay. Betty creates plates, cups, vases, planters, and many more items and bakes them in her kiln outside.

If you are partial to customized jewellery or just enjoy seeing creative work, stop in at Unique Bathsheba, also in Benalto.

Evarts, south of Highway #11 on Spruceview Road, was the original stopover for freight wagons travelling between Red Deer and Rocky Mountain House in the early 1900's. The only evidence that Evarts ever existed is the Historical Cairn. The plaque reads:

Historical Cairn, Evarts

This cairn is dedicated to honour of the pioneers of Evarts and District who arrived between 1900 and 1925 and also in honour of settlers outside the boundaries of the school district who contributed to the development of our area. Their courage, foresight, and perseverance established the basis of our agricultural community.

The inscription also lists the names of stores, blacksmith shops, restaurants, creameries, the hotel and its operator, the barbershop, the sawmill, livery barns, and freight haulers.

LESLIEVILLE

As you near the junction of Highway #761, slow down and search the field north of the highway for a long row of rusted, antique, farm machinery. The line heads northeast from the farmyard on the corner and is almost hidden by tall hay. The collection was begun many years ago, and each year more relics are added.

Follow #761 north for 3.2 kilometres (two miles), then turn east and drive 200 metres to the Spokeshave. The owner, Carl Sewell, designs custom furniture, repairs antiques, and does solid wood turnings. Canadian maple, birch, pine, and some specialty wood like black maple and cherry wood are the only materials Mr. Sewell uses for his handiwork.

Further north at Leslieville, the annual Central Alberta Antique and Model Show is staged in early August. The show has demonstrations of the machinery's role on the farm. After you have seen the machinery in action, relax and enjoy the Fiddler's Jamboree.

Rocky Mountain House and District

ROCKY MOUNTAIN HOUSE

Rocky Mountain House was established in 1799 by the North West Company as its most westerly and southerly fort in Blackfoot country. Because of the possibility of attacks, it was one of the most heavily fortified posts in Alberta. The Hudson's Bay Company soon constructed Acton House, close to its rival's post. Thirty-six years later, two new posts were built downstream from the original ones.

To honour this history, Alberta's first and only National Historic Park was developed seven kilometres (four miles) west of Rocky Mountain House on Highway #11A. Exhibits depict the life of the Plains and David Thompson. Artifacts from the fur trade, outmoded surveying equipment, and items from excavations of the forts are on display in the interpretive centre.

From the centre, two trails lead to the separate sites of forts. Take the time to walk down both. Along the trails are wooden structures with recorded messages and illustrations. These recordings were the first ones of their kind put into use by the Canadian Parks Service; they operate on solar power.

The short trail is about 0.9 kilometres (0.6 miles) long and will guide you to the location of the two forts inhabited from 1835-1875. Two chimneys, reconstructed from the rocks of the originals, stand in the trees. Near them is a Red River cart and a fur press.

The other trail is about 2.5 kilometres (1.5 miles) long. The walk is through the trees along the river bank. At intervals are pictures of plants or bushes with an explanation of their uses. When you come to a "Y" in the path, take the left fork to the York boat. At the boat, there are two teepees and an interpreter dressed in period clothing who will demonstrate the drying of meat for pemmican, candle making, beadwork, and making bannock. You can sample the food or roll up your sleeves and pitch in with the work.

Continue along the path to a picnic area, the canoe launch, a viewing platform from which you can see a herd of buffalo, and the site of the earlier Hudson's Bay Company and North West Company forts.

The Fur Trader's Freezer

Ice houses were built in the winter to store buffalo meat traded from the Natives or shot by the men at the fort. A square hole, large enough to hold over 500 buffalo carcasses, was dug. The men then cut ice from the river into blocks of equal sizes and laid them on the floor. Water was poured over them to freeze them together. More large cubes of ice were stacked for the walls and they, too, were drenched in water. • The carcasses, minus the head and feet were quartered without being skinned and piled in layers to the top of the pit. They were covered with a thick coating of straw, then a wooden shed was set on top. The meat froze and stayed that way long into the summer.

If you would like to experience the life of a voyageur after you have traversed the historic park, contact Voyageur Adventure Tours in Rocky Mountain House. They offer half day, full day, and overnight excursions. On each, you get a traditional canoe ride down the North Saskatchewan. Other activities depend on the length of the trip.

Mandelin Antique Musem, Rocky Mountain House

You may have seen the Mandelin Antique Museum in the midway of an exhibition or fair somewhere in Alberta. But if you haven't, stop in and see it during your stay at Rocky Mountain House. It is situated 16 kilometres (10 miles) south-west of the town on Highway #752. The museum is in a travelling trailer and there are telephones, radios, antique stoves, and various phonographs. One phonograph, made in the early 1900s, is called the Bing Pygmyphone and is one of the smallest in the world. A barbed wire display has some wires dating back to the late 1800s.

There are many craft shops in and around Rocky Mountain House. For handmade pottery, visit Craft Connections on Mainstreet. Fourteen kilometres (8.6 miles) south of Highway #11 on Highway #22 is Breezy Hill Farms, which specializes in wool gifts. They have saddlepads, wooden chair pads, and sheepskin slippers. Try their vehicle seat cover, which will keep you cool in summer and warm in winter.

To see native beadwork visit Tonto's Treasures at 5411 54th Street or phone 845-2479. Another stop should be the little shop in the Walking Eagle Inn. Here, you will find crafts done in traditional Native fashion..

Rocky Mountain House has a variety of summer and winter activities. There is the demolition derby in July and the Mountain Mud-fling in September.

About one kilometre north of the town is another large glacial erratic like the "Big Rock" near Okotoks. Alexander Henry mentioned it in his journals almost 200 years ago — the first documentation of this type of rock in North America.

CRIMSON LAKE PROVINCIAL PARK

For those visiting in the winter, the Winterfest is held on the last weekend in January at Crimson Lake Provincial Park. Events include bike, trike, and snowmobile races on the ice, non-studded, two-man quad (four wheel, all terrain vehicle) races, dog sled racing, the Mad Trapper events, and a local cutter parade with decorated horse-drawn sleighs. Children can take part in the one dog, kid-and-mutt race.

In the Rocky Mountain House area, parkland is gradually being replaced by boreal forest containing a large number of bogs and fens. Crimson Lake Provincial Park has a number of these bogs and fens in the low regions and aspen and lodgepole pine in the upland sections. Water and pygmy shrews, bog lemmings, and wolves inhabit the park.

Lodgepole pine

Bogs

Bogs of various dimensions range throughout the Northern Hemisphere. Formed when huge blocks of glacial ice melted, these pools had neither an inlet of fresh water nor a suitable drainage system and were called kettle hole lakes. Over many years, silt and partially decayed plants and animals accumulated on the bottom of the lakes and the water became shallower. A mat of vegetation was created on the surface, by shrubs and grass-like plants called sedges or when water willow branches creating a tangled mass floated on the water. Moss and other plants grew on this network and the result was a floating carpet. • A bog is in a state of perpetual, slow change. As the moss and plants die, they became compressed by the weight of water and newer plant life, and are slowly converted into layers of peat. A strong, pungent odor, caused by the constant decaying process, permeates the area. • Because of a shortage of oxygen and peat acids, few organisms live in the lower depths of the bog. In the 1950s, the body of a man was discovered by peat cutters in the Tollund Bog in Denmark. He was perfectly preserved with even his whiskers intact. After careful examination, it was determined that he had been submerged in the bog for two thousand years. •Fens, open bodies of water in the bog interior, help maintain the water table in the area and provide a habitat for small animals and birds.

Nordegg and District

There are many campsites on the David Thompson Highway between Rocky Mountain House and Banff National Park. For those who wish to canoe or raft on the North Saskatchewan River, there are launch sites indicated by signs. The first is at about kilometre 27 (mile 16.7), the second at about kilometre 63 (mile 39).

Half way between Rocky Mountain House and Nordegg, you get your first glimpse of the mountains. West of Nordegg you begin your drive through the mountains on a winding highway.

NORDEGG

Martin Nordegg came to Alberta from Germany to locate exploitable minerals for a large German corporation. He found coal in the Kananaskis, near Brazeau and Bighorn, and then discovered a new field west of Rocky Mountain House. He opened a mine and established a town called Nordegg. The town had 3,500 residents at its peak and the mine produced 900,000 metric tons (10 million tons) of coal over the years.

Nordegg's prosperity ended in the 1950s, when railroads switched to diesel fuel and coal was no longer in demand. The town was deserted until 1963, when the Alberta Government began using some buildings as a minimum security prison.

Restoration of the town and mine site has been undertaken in an effort to preserve the historic value of Nordegg. Because of the prison, you can only see the preserved buildings by guided tour, which begins at the Nordegg Heritage centre — a two-storey, white building at the southwest end of town.

RAM RIVER FALLS AND CRESCENT FALLS

To see the Ram River Falls, head west of Nordegg and turn south at Highway #940 (Forestry Trunk road). The gravel road is narrow, winding, and hilly, so do not expect to travel very fast. The scenery is great, with mountains, rivers valleys, and meadows. At about kilometre 11 (mile 6.8) you cross the North Saskatchewan river and at kilometre 27 (mile 16.7) is the North Ram River Recreation Area. Fifty-nine kilometres (36.5 miles) from the junction is the Ram River Falls and campground.

Ram River Falls

Drive past the first camping area to the second and park in the lot. Walk down the gravel path to the fence and the steps leading down to the viewpoint. It is a steep descent but you can see the falls all the way down. Water crashes down both sides of an outcrop of rock.

To see another waterfall, drive about 20 kilometres (12 miles) west from Nordegg, on the David Thompson Highway, to the road to Crescent Falls and Bighorn Canyon. The road is narrow and steep and after about three kilometres (1.9 miles) you come to a

Crescent Falls

viewpoint overlooking the Big Horn Canyon. Stop and take a look down at the river. When you come to a "Y" in the road, take the left fork and you will end up at the river above the falls. Climb the hill behind the fence and you will have a great view of the water rushing over the falls.

ABRAHAM LAKE

In 1972, the Big Horn Dam was constructed and Abraham Lake, the longest man-made lake in Alberta, was created. It was named after Siles Abraham, a Stoney who resided in the area for many years. The 32 kilometre (20 mile) long dam is one of the largest earth-filled dams in western Canada, and tours of the generating station are available.

Michener Mountain at Abraham Lake

The turquoise lake, with colourful mountains behind it, is a photographer's dream. One of the mountains is Michener Mountain, named after Roland Michener (see *Chapter 8*, Devon to Lacombe section). You can see it from a roadside turnout along the lake. Because of high winds on the lake, canoeing and boating are not recommended.

The David Thompson Resort, 26 kilometres (16 miles) west of Crescent Falls, has a large hotel with a spa, heated pool, and colour satellite television. Across the highway is McKenzie's Trail West, where you can rent horses for trail rides.

Sixteen kilometres (10 miles) west of the resort there is a road side turnout with an historic sign giving the history of the

Kootenay Plains, which are on both sides of the highway. There is also a plaque commemorating the official opening of the David Thompson Highway by Hon. Hugh Horner, MD., Deputy Premier, and Minister of Transportation, on August 3, 1975.

One-quarter kilometre from the sign is a parking lot and the beginning of the trail to Siffleur Falls. The falls are four kilometres (2.5 miles) from the lot. After about one kilometre on the trail, you arrive at a suspension bridge over the North Saskatchewan River. Anyone who has seen the brown river further along on its journey will marvel at the beautiful turquoise colour that it is here. Cross the bridge and follow the hiking signs to the falls.

From the falls you can continue into the Siffleur Wilderness Area, but only experienced wilderness hikers should attempt this journey. Contact the Alberta Forest Service in Rocky Mountain House for more information before you depart.

There are many guides and outfitters who offer horseback tours of the region and into the Bighorn Wildland Recreation Area. Whether you are looking for an hour's ride, a 12-day pack trip, good fishing, or a trophy animal, it is safest to enter the vast woodland with an experienced guide.

Beautiful scenery in Rocky Mountains.

Index

I • J

K • L

M

N

O

P

Further Reading

Breuer, Michael. *Historic Alberta*. Don Mills: Oxford, 1986.

Broadfoot, Barry. *Pioneer Years*. Toronto: Doubleday, 1976.

Brown, Craig, Ed. *The Illustrated History of Canada*. Toronto: Lester and Orpen Dennys, 1987.

Callwood, June. *Portrait of Canada*. New York: Doubleday, 1981.

The Canadian Encyclopedia. Edmonton: Hurtig, 1988.

Chalmer, Ernest. *Royal North-West Mounted Police*. Toronto: Coles, 1972.

Chatenay, Henri. *The Country Doctors*. Red Deer: Mattrix, 1980.

Colley, Kate Brighty. *While Rivers Flow*. Saskatoon: Western Producer Prairie, 1970.

Conway, J. *The West*. Toronto: Lorimer, 1983.

Dempsey, Hugh. *The Best From Alberta*. Saskatoon: Western Producer Prairie, 1981.

—, ed. *The Best of Alberta History*. Saskatoon: Western Producer Prairie, 1981.

Fryer, Harold. *Alberta — The Pioneer Years*. Langley: Stagecoach, 1979.

—. *Ghost Towns of Alberta*. Langley: Mr. Paperback, 1981.

Hamilton, Jacques. *Our Alberta Heritage*. Calgary: Calgary Power, 1978.

Hardy, W.G., ed. *Alberta, A Natural History*. Edmonton: Hurtig, 1977.

—, ed. *The Alberta Golden Jubilee Anthology*. Toronto: McClelland and Stewart, 1955.

Helgason, Gail. *The First Albertans*. Edmonton: Lone Pine, 1987.

Hocking, Anthony. *Alberta*. Scarborough: McGraw, 1979.

Holmgren, Eric and Patricia. *Over 2000 Place Names of Alberta*. Saskatoon: Western Producer Prairie, 1976.

Kidd, Robert. *Fort George*. Edmonton: Provincial Museum and Archives, 1970.

Lussier, A.S., ed. *Louis Riel and the Métis*. Winnipeg: Pemmican, 1983.

MacBeth, Reverend. *Making of the Canadian West*. Rexdale: Coles, 1973. Originally published in 1898.

MacDonald, Robert. *Owners of Eden*. Ballantree, 1974.

MacGregor, James. *Blankets and Beads*. Edmonton: Institute of Applied Arts, 1949.

—. *A History of Alberta*. Edmonton: Hurtig, 1977.

Meyers, Jay. *Canadian Facts and Dates*. Don Mills: Fitzhenry and Whiteside, 1985.

Morse, Eric. *Fur Trade Canoe Routes of Canada*. Ottawa: Morton, Baslaw & Co, 1968.

Newman, Peter. *Caesars of the Wilderness*. Harmondsworth: Viking, 1987.

—. *Company of Adventurers*. Harmondsworth: Viking, 1985.

Palmer, T. & H. *Peoples of Alberta*. Saskatoon: Western Producer Prairie, 1985.

Paterson, T.W. *Canadian Battles and Massacres*. Langley: Stagecoach, 1977.

Provincial Museum and Archives, Edmonton.

Robotti, P. and F. *Keys to Gracious Living*. Toronto: Prentice-Hall, 1972.

Sheppe, Walter, ed. *First Man West*. Los Angeles: U of California P, 1962.

Silverman, Elaine. *The Last Best West*. Montreal: Eden Press, 1984.

Spalding, David, ed. *A Nature Guide to Alberta*. Edmonton: Hurtig, 1980.

Time Life Books. *The Canadians*. Virginia, 1979.

Woodcock, George. *The Canadians*. Don Mills: Fitzhenry & Whiteside, 1979.